MW00745163

The *Parents*™ Magazine Baby and Childcare Series combines the most up-to-date medical findings, the advice of doctors and child psychologists, and the actual day-to-day experiences of parents like you. Covering a wide variety of subjects, these books answer all your questions, step by important step, and provide the confidence of knowing you're doing the best for your child —with help from *Parents*™ Magazine.

Other *Parents*™ Childcare Books
Published by Ballantine Books:

PARENTS™ BOOK FOR YOUR BABY'S FIRST YEAR

PARENTS™ BOOK OF CHILDHOOD ALLERGIES

PARENTS™ BOOK OF BREAST-FEEDING

PARENTS™ BOOK OF PREGNANCY AND BIRTH

PARENTS™ BOOK OF BABY NAMES

PARENTS™ BOOK FOR THE TODDLER YEARS

PARENTS™ BOOK FOR RAISING A HEALTHY CHILD

PARENTS™ BOOK FOR NEW FATHERS

PARENTS™ BOOK OF TOILET TEACHING

Parents™
Book of
Infant
Colic

PHYLLIS SCHNEIDER

BALLANTINE BOOKS • NEW YORK

The author would like to thank the parents who granted lengthy—and candid—interviews for this book. Special thanks also go to Laura Grill for her help in locating information on the elusive subject of colic and to Evelyn Podsiadlo for her expert editorial advice and support.

Library of Congress Catalog Card Number: 89-91795

ISBN 0-345-35103-7

Manufactured in the United States of America

First Edition: January 1990

Contents

Introduction

In the fall of 1984, my husband, Ted, and I adopted a four-month-old baby girl. Like most new parents we fully expected to learn the basics of baby care by trial and error (and with a little help from numerous magazine articles and books we'd read). At first, all was well. Brooke was alert and active, ate well and slept soundly—and she "cried on cue"—that is, whenever she was wet or hungry or needed to be entertained. In short, she appeared to be the "perfect baby."

But two weeks after her arrival, our unusually placid infant suddenly took on a Jekyll-and-Hyde personality. She was fine during the day, but at 5:00 P.M., almost to the minute, she'd begin to wail, then scream piteously, angrily, her tiny mouth forming a "square," her lips turning purple, her tongue furled upward. The baby, who a few hours earlier had been content to nestle up against me, now went rigid, her arms flailing,

1

her body tense and shaking. She was inconsolable—and so was I! The night of Brooke's first "attack" I was certain she must be terribly ill, since her face was flushed and her body overheated, but when she finally stopped crying at 9:00 P.M. and fell asleep, she cooled down almost instantly.

The next day the baby was happy and active, so I put off calling her pediatrician; after all, I didn't want to be accused of being a "hysterical mother" when Brooke seemed absolutely healthy in every other way. But at five that evening, the baby let out a piercing scream and she was off again on another four-hour tangent of sobbing. I tried everything I knew to comfort her. I bounced her on my knee. I put her tummy-down on a warm hot-water bottle (her abdomen seemed distended, but she hadn't passed any gas). I strapped her in the mechanical infant swing she usually delighted in and watched as she swung and screamed, swung and screamed. Finally I called a friend who suggested that Brooke must have "colic." I knew almost nothing about the condition; like most people, I assumed colic was a gastrointestinal problem and that colicky babies simply had enormous amounts of gas. We'd been feeding Brooke a cow's-milk infant formula and I wondered if that might be causing her problems, but she'd been taking the formula for the previous two weeks, so I ruled out an allergy.

True to form, Brooke was content the next morning, chipper and ready to play with her rattle and a squishy bear she particularly liked. The day progressed as usual and Brooke whimpered only when she was wet or hungry. Then, at 5:00 P.M., I heard an ominous whine, and I braced myself, expecting the worst. Within minutes, the baby was red in the face and wailing and gasping for air, her little hands curled into tight fists, her legs pulled up to her belly as though she were in pain. All my previous attempts to comfort her had failed, so I merely picked her up and walked around the house as she screamed and writhed. At 8:00 P.M., our neighbor, Laura, called to ask if "everything was all right." Obviously, she'd heard the baby's relentless, agonized screams and I'm sure she must have wondered if I was torturing the poor, innocent child! I assured Laura that everything was "under control," but that Brooke had been screaming for several hours and I assumed she just had a simple case of colic. When I hung up the phone, I held Brooke out in front of me and demanded, "Why are you doing this to me?" At that point I had never felt so *out* of control.

Quickly I dialed Ted's work number. "If you don't come home instantly and take care of this baby, one of us might not survive the evening!" I shouted, then slammed down the phone. Ted must have been alarmed by the tone of my voice because he was home within twenty minutes, instead of his usual thirty! He took one look at me—frazzled—and then at Brooke —sweaty and tired, but still managing hoarse, croaking screams—put the baby over his shoulder, patted her firmly on the back, and she let out a thunderous burp. She was as startled as we were by the sudden, deep noise, and she looked around happily and gurgled.

"Why, nothing's wrong with her," Ted insisted. "She just had a little gas!"

As it turned out, our daughter did *not* have colic, a condition that always begins within the first few weeks after birth, not at four months. She was merely experiencing a severe gastrointestinal upset caused by the iron-fortified formula we'd recently switched her to, and once we started her on regular formula (with an easily digested iron supplement prescribed by her pediatrician) she was fine. But for three days I got a first-hand taste of what it's like to be the parent of a colicky baby.

When your child screams nonstop, you initially feel empathy, but eventually empathy changes to frustration, which can easily turn into all-out anger at the baby. Parents of colicky children report roller-coaster emotions. On the one hand, they want to comfort and help their baby. But on the other, they're tempted to get as far away from the miserable, squalling child as possible! After all, parenting a newborn is a tremendously tiring proposition, but caring for a colicky baby is exhausting both emotionally and physically.

As the parent of a colicky child, it's likely you get little or no sleep. Your nerves are on edge. You don't think clearly. You're irritable and cranky, and understandably so. You may move through the day as though you're sleepwalking. Getting dressed in the morning (after your baby has kept you up for seven hours straight) is a monumental task. And while people may sympathize with your situation, they can't possibly understand what you're going through.

Although my daughter had "pseudocolic"—and it was blessedly short-lived—the few evenings I listened to her agonized screams allowed me to understand the tremendous challenge parents of colicky babies face. That's why I've written this book; I know what you're going through and I want to reassure you that you're not alone. Millions of other weary parents have struggled through a child's colicky months, wondering if the turmoil would ever end. Like these parents, you want to learn all the best ways to calm a baby who's out of control, who won't stop shrieking, and in chapter 6 we've listed dozens of the most effective methods of managing a colic attack; these are safe, simple, tried-and-true "remedies" that have worked for other parents. Of course, you'll be tempted to skip forward to that chapter. Go ahead! Coping with colic is akin to fighting a war, and you need all the best tactical maneuvers at your fingertips.

But in dealing with infant colic, it's also very helpful to understand why babies cry in the first place and what their cries tell us, as well as how doctors diagnose colic, and what causes this perplexing condition. So be sure to backtrack to chapters 1, 2, and 4.

Because a number of parents interviewed for this book felt their children's doctors either weren't sympathetic or didn't really understand themselves just what triggers colic attacks—or the best ways to control them—chapter 3 tells how to communicate with your pediatrician as well as how to elicit her support—even if she just lends a sympathetic ear now and then as you describe the ordeal you and your baby are enduring.

Other chapters touch on the myriad myths surrounding colic (for example, that "too much fresh air" precipitates colic attacks or that colicky babies grow into difficult children); whether colic has any long-term physical or emotional effects on children; and, perhaps most important, the effect a colicky baby has on his parents. "Taking Care of Yourself," chapter 7, gives down-to-earth advice on surviving the rough, exhausting colic months. All too often, we tend to focus entirely on our child, when we really need to stop and take stock of our own health and emotional needs. Caring for yourself is almost, if not as important as nurturing your colicky baby.

As you read this book—and face the challenging weeks and months ahead—keep in mind that you *will* survive. And your baby will not only survive, he'll thrive. Finally, remind yourself again and again that colic is a short-lived condition, that the end is in sight (even though your view may be temporarily clouded!), and one morning you will wake up to find that your unhappy, wailing baby has metamorphosed into a contented, cuddly, loving child.

1. Why Babies Cry

In the months before your baby's birth, you probably spent many pleasurable hours fantasizing about him. It's likely you pictured your baby as being close to perfect, a healthy, contented infant who would sleep peacefully for hours, eat heartily and happily, smile charmingly at you whenever you bent over his crib— and, of course, cry a little when he needed to be fed or changed or merely comforted.

If you're the parent of a colicky baby, those fantasies quickly evaporate. Far from seeming content, your baby looks as though he's in excruciating pain much of the time. He may eat ravenously, but then he'll draw his little legs up to his belly and clench his fists, often flailing his tiny arms frantically. His face reddens, his lips turn blue, and he cries—or shrieks agonizingly— for hours on end, totally inconsolable. When he finally falls asleep, too weak and exhausted to utter another whimper, you, too, are drained, physically and emotionally.

Coping with infant crying is one of the toughest challenges any parent faces. Coping with *colicky* crying is ten times more difficult, and it's only natural that you may feel helpless and frustrated. What's more, you may feel as though you lack an adequate support system: most parents of noncolicky babies won't be able to relate to your dilemma. Your relatives will offer tips on comforting a "fussy" child, but until they spend twenty-four hours—or, better yet, a week—with your "high-needs" baby, they can't come close to realizing the extreme stress you're under. Even your baby's pediatrician might not fully grasp just how overwhelmed, tired, anxious, and even resentful you may be at this point, how "out of control" you feel.

Learning as much as you can about infant colic will help you regain some sense of control over your life—and your baby's welfare—during the tumultuous months that lie ahead. In this book we'll discuss the various theories about the possible causes of infant colic as well as the many ways to manage your baby's colic while it lasts (and safeguard your sanity in the process!). But in caring for the colicky baby, it's also helpful to take a close look at the dynamics of infant crying in general, to discover why babies cry, what they're trying to tell us through their wails, whimpers, and sobs, and perhaps most important, to understand just how dramatically an infant's cries can affect her parents.

Your baby's first language: In the first days and weeks after her birth, your baby is at the most helpless, vulnerable stage in her life, and she depends on you to meet her every need, to make sure she's dry and clean, warm and well fed and comforted. Her cry is the most effective way she has of communicating those needs to you, her way of telling you what she requires to live. An infant's cry is, truly then, an expression of survival. Its purpose is to elicit an immediate response from you—and perhaps that's why nature has designed it to sound unpleasant, even harsh and grating, to the human ear. Because a cry "cries to be turned off," parents tend to respond quickly and consistently to their baby's cry.

Crying is a normal part of your baby's twenty-four-hour sleep/wake cycle and during the first weeks of life, a cry usually signals the onset of wakefulness. Newborns generally sleep between twelve and eighteen hours a day, though some will doze for up to twenty-two hours. At first, a baby drifts in and out of sleep and waking states, with very brief alert periods interspersed. During these alert/wakeful times, your baby may try to focus on your face or a colorful toy in her crib, or she might just listen to the sound of your voice. Her central nervous system is just beginning to mature, so she's having difficulty processing all the external stimuli around her, the clatter of dishes in the kitchen, music coming from the stereo in the next room, a ray of sunlight glimmering through her nursery window, and one of the most natural ways of controlling those stimuli is to shut them out, to fall asleep.

Over the next three months, your baby will become increasingly able to handle stimulation, and at the same time her periods of alertness and attention will become longer and more frequent. Rather than crying the moment she wakens, she might shift directly into a "quiet" alert state for a few minutes or even longer before telling you through her wail that she's hungry or wet or merely needs to feel your loving arms around her.

But during the first few weeks of life, while her central nervous system "settles into place," her crying will be reflexive in nature. That is, she'll have no control over the why and when of her crying. She's merely aware that something is bothering her, that she's wet or her tummy is empty and hurts (though she's still too young to differentiate between these uncomfortable feelings)—and her brain sends a signal triggering the cry response, a sudden intake of air, then the expiration or wail. As she approaches eight weeks her cry will change dramatically. No longer just a reflexive response to a message from her brain, your baby's cries are now becoming more voluntary in nature. Even at this tender age, a baby has a rudimentary understanding of cause and effect, and she realizes that when she cries, something will happen, that someone will change her diaper or feed her or bundle her up for a stroll around the block. It's at this point that parents begin to perceive an emotional quality in their child's various cries, and rather than assuming that a short burst of sobs means your baby's hungry or wet or in pain, you may catch yourself saying, "Oh, I know *that* cry, she's *mad*!" or "I think she wants attention, a little cuddling."

Some experts feel this new, voluntary control over crying provides the infant with valuable experience that will help him master the important noncry vocalizations, such as gurgling, babbling, and cooing, sounds that appear at around three months and lead to later language development. Through crying, your baby is also becoming aware of his tongue and mouth, and he's now able to experiment with a new "vocabulary" of babbles and coos by pressing his tongue against the roof of his mouth to create these fascinating sounds. As your baby gets older he'll begin to cry for shorter periods, and by nine months his cries will become "speechlike" in terms of rate and rhythm. These shorter cries resemble the length of syllables and words.

Normal patterns of crying: Each baby is unique and so is his cry. If your baby's cry were recorded on a sound spectrograph—a sophisticated instrument equipped with a pen that "draws" the acoustics of the cry on a revolving drum—the resulting "cry print" would be as individual to your child as his fingerprints. Similarly, every baby has his own cry *style*. Some babies cry sporadically throughout the day, others save their sobs for the hectic evening hours. Some babies are easily consoled, others need a great deal of attention. Some babies cry a little, others a lot. And although the parents of a child who cries nonstop every day for three or more hours might naturally wonder if something is drastically wrong with their baby, it's likely that he's perfectly healthy. (Certain cries do signal abnormalities, however, and doctors use sound spectrographs and computers to analyze the cries of infants they suspect are ill. By examining the acoustics of cries, doctors are now able to diagnose numerous conditions, including brain damage, meningitis, chromosomal abnormalities such as Down's syndrome, and endocrine disorders. Cry analysis is even being used to predict which children might be susceptible to sudden infant death syndrome, and some researchers feel that one day all newborn infants will be routinely screened through this noninvasive procedure to identify or predict any medical problems.)

Ironically, while the infant who spends much of his day screaming at the top of his lungs may be entirely healthy, the baby who doesn't cry at all is actually the one parents should worry about. Babies who don't cry, who are unusually apathetic or passive, may be suffering from a serious emotional or physical disorder.

The first major study on infant crying was conducted at the Mayo Clinic in 1945. A group of researchers observed seventy-two babies in a newborn nursery, tracking each child for twenty-four hours a day. The observers recorded the onset of each crying spell and the duration. If there was an apparent reason for the crying (wetness, hunger, uncomfortable position) it was recorded. Most of the newborns cried between one and eleven minutes per hour. The maximum amount of crying per day was 243 minutes. The minimum was forty-eight minutes and the total average of crying per day was about two hours.

The researchers attributed 36 percent of the infants' cries to hunger, 21 percent to wet diapers, 8 percent to soiled diapers. The surprising discovery was that 35 percent—or more than one-third—of the babies' cries couldn't be attributed to any discernible cause, and the researchers could only guess at what may have triggered this unexplained fussing: a reaction to the bright lights or loud noises in the nursery, painful contractions in the digestive system, or possibly, the infants' need for cuddling and rhythmic motion.

An important study by pediatrician T. Berry Brazelton in 1962 expanded on the Mayo research. Brazelton asked parents of eighty infants to keep detailed diaries of their babies' crying habits and what emerged was a fairly consistent evolution of cry patterns during an infant's first three months. Only twelve of the eighty babies cried for less than one-and-a-half hours a day while half cried for at least two hours. By the age of six weeks, the crying peaked at an average of three hours a day. At twelve weeks, it decreased to one hour a day. Like the Mayo researchers, Brazelton also found that nearly all of the babies cried for unexplained reasons.

Brazelton pointed out that the colicky cry pattern seems to mimic the "normal/fussy" cry pattern of the infants he studied, at least in the usual three-month duration. Typically, colic begins between three days to three weeks after a baby's birth and rages fairly steadily for approximately three months (some cases continue for four, five, or even six months), then either tapers off gradually or ends suddenly. In both instances, the crying—colicky or "normal/fussy"—subsides at the same time the infant's central nervous system has matured to the point that he's more capable of handling external stimulation as well as soothing himself with calming techniques like thumb or finger sucking or focusing for long periods on an interesting mobile or toy. Because both colicky and normal/fussy crying tend to disappear at three months of age, some experts have suggested that colic is merely "a lot of normal crying."

The evening breakdown: Brazelton also found that at the age of six weeks over half of the infants in his study cried for predictable periods at the end of the day (as we'll see later, colicky crying often occurs during the late afternoon and evening hours). The crying typically began with a whimper, and if the baby was picked up, changed, talked to or held, he might stop fussing for a few seconds or minutes, but invariably he'd begin to cry again. The crying increased in intensity over the next one-and-a-half hours and the babies seemed inconsolable, but after their crying jags they would eat well and sleep soundly.

Parents noted in their diaries that this unexplained, end-of-the-day wailing usually coincided with the excitement that built up as the mother or father returned home from work. The dinner hour is a stressful time in most families. Older children are hungry and pleading for snacks, either Mom or Dad is trying to prepare dinner and pay attention to the new baby at the same time, and someone has probably turned on the television as well as a few lamps here and there. Suddenly the baby's world is flooded with all sorts of sights and sounds.

Brazelton concluded that many babies struggle to maintain an active alert state during the day, attempting to respond to their parents and take in everything that is happening around them. When evening approaches, they work extra hard, trying to concentrate on everything in their exciting new world, and ultimately they become exhausted, their nervous systems "overload" (like a computer that's been fed too much information), and they literally break down for a time, crying uncontrollably to relieve pent-up tension.

In this respect, babies are no different from adults, who, after a hard day of work need to unwind by jogging, swimming, or merely blanking out in front of the TV set. But, of course, your baby can't dash out for a jog at 5:30 when he's feeling exhausted and stressed, so he has to rely on his only method of releasing tension—crying. (Many adults will say, too, that they feel immensely better after a "good cry," and research lends credence to their claim. The very act of crying, according to scientists, is an effective method of expressing emotion and relieving stress. In fact, the shedding of emotional tears seems to play a direct role in alleviating stress according to the most recent studies. Several chemicals, including endorphins, the body's natural pain-relieving and mood-elevating substances, have been isolated in tear secretions. It may be that tears, like sweat and urine, cleanse the body of toxic substances that accumulate during stressful times.)

Does temperament play a role in crying? "He was such a good baby, easy from the start," says Anne, talking about her son, Daniel. "He cried, but as soon as he began to nurse or I held him close, he quieted down. Even today at eight months, if he begins to fuss, I just pick him up and carry him on my hip while I'm doing my work around the house and he calms down quickly." Daniel is, clearly, the epitome of the "placid" baby.

Maria, on the other hand, describes her son, Mark, as "tense from the beginning. At just a few days of age, he startled easily; a slight noise or tiny beam of light would waken him and he'd begin to scream, his arms rigid and shaking. Nothing we did seemed to soothe him. Mark is two and a half now, and although he's perfectly normal in every respect, he's still a tense and somewhat serious child."

Two different babies, two entirely different temperaments.

As parents it's only natural that we want to define our babies' personalities. We call them "easygoing" or "tense and irritable" or "good some of the time, cranky at others." It's not that we're labeling our children, we're merely trying to figure out where they fit on the easy-baby/difficult-baby scale, and, perhaps, we're also looking ahead, attempting to determine whether our fussy or colicky three-week-old will turn out to be a hard-to-handle two-year-old!

Your baby's inborn temperament is evident as early as the first day after he's born. In fact, researchers, using sophisticated temperament assessment scales, are able to measure a newborn's temperament fairly accurately. Among other things, they observe the baby to see how quickly and easily she adapts to repeated sounds, especially when she's trying to fall asleep. They will observe how quickly she becomes excited, measuring changes in skin color (an indication of excitement), and how rapidly she moves from sleep to alert states or from sleep to crying. And, perhaps most important, they note how consolable she is when distressed. Does she need a lot of help from a parent or nurse in order to stop crying? Or can she soothe herself by focusing on a colorful pattern in her crib bumper?

Of course, early temperament assessments aren't absolute predictors of the type of personality your baby will develop over the coming months or years (temperament can be more accurately measured between four and eight months when the baby's central nervous system is working efficiently and his responses are more stable). And babies who are "difficult" for the first six months or so don't necessarily turn into handfuls as toddlers or preschoolers. In fact, many tense babies develop calmer temperaments in later infancy. On the other hand, some placid babies go on to become little terrors as they approach toddlerhood.

But babies are, indeed, born with their own distinct temperament (long gone are the days when a newborn's personality was viewed as a blank canvas to be "painted" by his parents!). And there's little doubt that temperament does influence how much a baby cries. Some babies are active and tense at birth and they cry a great deal. They just naturally possess a low threshold for receiving and responding to external stimulation. They startle at the slightest sound or lightest touch, they wail the minute they sense they're wet or hungry, they waken almost instantly if a dim light is flicked on in their nursery. And after working all day to maintain an alert state, they're likely to launch into an evening tirade. Often perceived as "difficult" or "irritable," this type of infant will be slow in responding to her parents' comforting caresses and cuddles. Rocking and carrying may not calm her once she's in the throes of a good cry. She's also less able than other babies to soothe herself, to distract herself from whatever's upsetting her by sucking on her thumb or fingers or focusing on the entrancing mobile hanging above her crib. A fussy baby, she cries frequently and for long periods and needs lots of consistent and patient attention from her parents.

Placid babies, on the other hand, have a high threshold for receiving external stimuli. While the tense baby may whimper the moment she's wet, the placid child often waits an hour or longer before telling you through his cry that he's starting to feel miserable. He can fall asleep anywhere, anytime—in the midst of a roomful of people or a brightly lit nursery or restaurant. When he feels overwhelmed by sights and sounds and a little too much loving attention from his family, he falls back on a fairly well-developed coping system for shutting out everything, soothing himself by thumb or finger sucking or merely curling up and falling asleep. This is a baby who's able to "turn off" when he's had enough! He's also easily calmed by being held or rocked and it's easy to nip his crying in the bud.

If you're the parent of a colicky baby, the first description of the irritable, super-sensitive infant will sound like it fits your child to a tee. But keep in mind that though some colicky babies are born with tense, difficult temperaments and go on to become perfectly normal, but active, intense toddlers, many colicky babies go through a metamorphosis when they emerge from their colicky state. It's not unusual to hear tales of colicky infants, babies who drove their parents to despair, who became easygoing, carefree babies at three or four months of age. As we'll see later, there's a very fine line between the fussy, irritable infant and the colicky baby, and sometimes it's almost impossible to distinguish one from the other. The important thing to remember is that during these first few months, your colicky baby is a high-needs child. That is, he'll require much the same constant, consistent, patient attention and understanding the fussy baby needs. He may just require that attention in double doses.

What your baby's cries mean: Parents, especially mothers, are very adept at identifying their own baby's cries from those of another child. Your baby's cry is made up of a unique set of sounds, with a distinct interplay of varying pitches and frequencies, and even a few days after your child's birth, you begin to tune in to his cries, becoming familiar with all the subtle—and not so subtle—nuances.

Mothers are also significantly better than fathers when it comes to distinguishing between different types of cries—the hunger cry and the pain cry, for instance—perhaps because mothers spend more time with their babies during the first few months. (Though fathers are playing an increasingly greater role in child rearing these days, the fact remains that few fathers have the luxury of a long parental leave of absence from work to spend time with their newborns. For the most part, it's Mom who, after listening to baby's whimpers and sobs all day long, becomes quickly familiar with the sounds that make up the different types of cries.)

Your baby's cries are her language, and by listening to the sound of each cry, you can determine what she needs. Although her cries are distinctly different from those of other babies, there are certain recognizable patterns in pitch, intensity, and duration in each of the cry types.

Pain cries begin suddenly and are generally high-pitched and shrill. The first cry is loud and long and is followed by a lengthy pause, then another screamlike cry. Your baby will cry with her whole body when she's in pain. Her mouth will open wide and may appear "square." Her lips may turn blue or purple and she'll furl her tongue upward. She may extend her arms and legs, then jerk them tensely back into her body again. The pain cry is the most intense of all baby cries, and parents often describe colicky crying as being very similar.

Hunger cries are less shrill than pain cries and usually begin with a short burst followed by a pause while baby catches her breath. It's almost as though your baby is giving you time to pick her up and put her to your breast or ready her bottle. Hunger cries can quickly turn into pain or anger cries, though, and once your baby's "gone over the hill," it may be difficult to calm her for a peaceful feeding. Before a hunger cry begins, you may notice certain precry cues, such as restlessness, sucking on fingers, or nuzzling at the breast.

Angry cries are sustained and have a vibrato quality. The pitch is generally lower than that of pain or hunger cries and the baby may sound hoarse since she's so mad she's actually forcing a lot of air out in her cry.

Bored cries are whiny and low-pitched, almost "moaning." A bored baby, who's lonely or has become uncomfortable lying or sitting in one position for too long, may tell you she needs some stimulation by whining or moaning, then go into several short bursts of crying (she may even stop crying suddenly, look around to see whether you're coming to her rescue, then start all over again).

Fatigue or tension-releasing cries start gradually, then build in intensity. Each cry is longer than the other and there's a wailing quality and a definite vibrato.

Cries during illness tend to be weepy and prolonged. They sound weak, whiny or nasal, and they're generally lower-pitched than the pain cry. "Pitiful" is how one mother described the cries of her feverish child.

How quickly we react to our child's cries depends to some extent on what he's telling us. If a baby starts to scream suddenly, signaling that he's in pain, our minds and bodies go into a red alert and we'll leap up from whatever we've been doing and rush to him. But if his cry tells us that he's hungry or bored or mad, we may take a little more time in responding since we automatically assume there's no emergency.

Although we quickly learn to interpret the meanings behind many of our baby's cries, often a mother or father will say, "I just don't know why he's crying a lot of the time. I've fed him, diapered him, and cuddled him—I've tried everything to calm this child and he's still crying! I feel as though I'm not getting through to him, or he's not able to communicate what he needs to me. I must be doing something wrong. I feel so guilty; I should be able to understand what my child wants."

When you feel that you aren't able to interpret your baby's cries accurately, if he seems to be crying "for no good reason," keep in mind that even the top researchers in infant crying aren't able to explain *all* of a baby's sobs. As we've seen, many babies spend up to a third of their cry time in unexplained fussing or screaming. It's important that you don't blame yourself for not being able to figure out what your child is trying to tell you. At these times, the best you can do is to make sure your child is dry and warm and fed and assured of your loving presence.

Exploding the "spoiled baby" myth: Not so long ago, behavioral psychologists warned parents to avoid responding too quickly or too often to their baby's cries, saying the parent would risk spoiling the child. In fact, they would unwittingly teach or condition him to cry more often to get what he wanted, and eventually the tiny infant would wield considerable power over his helpless folks. Even though recent research proves these claims totally untrue, the "spoiled baby" myth still persists, and you may find many a well-meaning relative or friend cautioning you to harden your heart and ignore your baby's cries, lest somewhere up the road you find yourself saddled with a whiny, weepy, clinging child who'll dictate your every move!

When your baby cries, he's not trying to manipulate you, he's merely telling you that he needs something. You won't spoil an infant by picking him up when he whimpers, nor will you teach him to cry more often to "get what he wants." On the contrary, numerous studies indicate that the more quickly and consistently parents respond to their baby—and the more they carry the baby—the less he'll cry in the long run.

Recently researchers at the Montreal Children's Hospital Institute studied ninety-nine mother-infant pairs, instructing half the parents to carry their babies in their arms or an infant carrier for no less than three hours a day; the other mothers were told to pick up and hold their babies as they normally would. The babies were between three and twelve weeks of age. It was found that the infants who were carried more cried 43 percent less overall and 51 percent less during the evening hours when measured at the peak crying age of six weeks. Similar, but smaller decreases occurred at four, eight, and twelve weeks.

As a result of the study, the researchers suggested that the relative lack of carrying in our society may predispose babies to increased crying—and even colic. They noted that in many non-Western cultures, where babies are carried in front- or backpacks or "slings" all day long while their mothers work, the infants cry very little. And in some of these countries, colic is virtually unheard of. Of course, a mother who carries her baby all day, or even three or more hours per day, is particularly attuned to the infant's body language. A squirming baby, tugging at his mother's breast, is obviously sending cues that he's hungry, and the mother can quickly prevent his cries by feeding him. But the rhythm and motion of carrying itself, as well as close body contact, are important, too. Rhythmic motion has a remarkably calming effect on a fussy baby.

Responding promptly now pays off later: By responding promptly and consistently to your baby during the crucial early months, you'll actually help him develop his noncrying mode of language and foster a sense of independence as well. Studies show that securely attached infants, those whose parents responded quickly to their cries, and who feel safe and well cared for, are more likely to use noncrying language—coos, babbles, gestures, and facial expressions—to communicate their needs by age one. And rather than turning into clingy, dependent little creatures, they're more independent than the insecurely attached babies, whose parents have ignored their cries or let them "cry it out" on a regular basis.

The securely attached one-year-old will eagerly explore his fascinating new world; that doesn't mean he won't still rely on you, of course, but you'll find you won't need to keep him constantly entertained. He'll be able to lose himself completely in play with his favorite toy, for instance, and he won't notice that you've left the room for a few minutes. What's more, by age two he'll tend to approach life more positively and fare better at problem-solving games as well as acquiring new skills, whereas the insecurely attached child is more likely to see life in a negative, distrustful manner, and she may give up more easily when faced with problem-solving games.

Experts feel that during the first weeks and months of your baby's life, you can help her develop a firm sense of trust by responding consistently to her cries. Gradually, she'll begin to anticipate your responses, to trust that you'll come to her aid, and by six months that anticipation time will increase even more as she learns to suppress her whimpers and wails.

But when a baby's parents regularly ignore her cries, she may react in one of two ways. She might begin to cry longer and more often, and her screams will take on an especially grating or disturbing sound. Or, sensing that when she cries no one comes, intuiting that her crying is to no avail, sooner or later she may just give up and become apathetic. In this type of situation, the parent/child relationship can be seriously undermined since the foundation for successful communication isn't developing properly. These cases are extreme, and those parents who find themselves ignoring their baby's cries most of the time, who feel constantly depressed or helpless—or just indifferent—because their child cries nonstop all day long, may benefit from counseling.

The power of a baby's cry: Your baby's wails have a profound effect on you, both physiologically and psychologically. When a nursing mother hears her baby begin to cry, certain hormones are released in her body, causing the skin over her breasts to increase rapidly in temperature and her milk to let down. If the baby's cry becomes too intense, however, turning into a pain or hunger cry, the mother may tense up and her milk won't come as easily.

At the sound of a baby's cry, both mothers and fathers experience accelerated heart rate, sweaty palms, and a rapid rise in blood pressure, all classic signals of the "fight or flight" response. Your first reaction may be to "fight," to stop the crying by some sort of intervention, be it changing your baby or feeding him or rocking him in your arms. When a baby's cries are intense, when he's shrieking with gusto or when his cries "go over the hill" and you have that sinking feeling nothing you do will calm him, your reaction may be one of "flight"—to get away from the annoying, perplexing, or heartrending sobs while your spouse, a friend, or a sitter takes over for a while and you escape to peace and quiet.

The purpose of a baby's cry is to get a quick response from someone, and for that reason the sound is extremely disturbing. An infant cry is twenty decibels higher than ordinary human speech and as irritating as busy street traffic noise or the sound of a jackhammer thirty-five feet away from you. It can cut through everything, your sleep, your conversation, your thought processes, and it's impossible to ignore. If there were an "ideal" cry, it would be disturbing enough to cause you to want to comfort your baby, to feel empathy toward her. But it shouldn't be so disturbing that it creates feelings of anger or helplessness in you. Unfortunately, most babies don't master the "ideal" cry! And when your baby goes into a crying jag you aren't able to quell, it's only natural that your first feelings of altruism toward your child may quickly turn into feelings of anger. Many parents have ambivalent feelings about their baby's cries, experiencing both empathy and hostility at the same time. A mother or father may have an overwhelming desire to order the baby to "just shut up," but at the same time, wish to comfort the child, to figure out what's behind his screams and remedy the problem.

Is baby putting us to the test? It's only natural, too, that when our baby cries we feel we're facing our first real "test" as parents. On the one hand, we might think the baby is telling us we're not doing our job right, that because we can't isolate the cause of his crying and do something about it, we just don't quite measure up! These feelings usually overtake us when we're particularly tired and frustrated by the demands of parenting and questioning whether we were ever cut out to care for a baby in the first place.

On the other hand, we may become angry at the child, viewing his cries as something he's "done," his first "bad" act. Though an infant has no intention or ability to manipulate, parents often want to control his crying, to stop it somehow, and this need for control can sometimes carry over into other areas of the parent/child relationship later on, setting the stage for power struggles during the toddler and preschool years. Experts feel that crying is one of the first and most important aspects of the developing parent/child relationship and how it's perceived and managed can have a definite impact on the way parents and kids interact for years to come.

Your reaction to your baby's cries: A steadily shrieking infant can test the mettle of even the most resilient parents. One mother says, "I never understood how someone could abuse a helpless little baby until I had a colicky child! I've never hurt my son, but I can really comprehend now how parents sometimes feel so pressured, so overwhelmed by twenty-four-hour crying, they can do something awful—especially if they don't have a spouse or relative to help out with the baby during the day."

Excessive crying is the most common reason given by parents who have abused their children when authorities ask what triggered the battering. And researchers have found that child abusers tend to respond differently to a crying infant than nonabusive parents. In one major study, a group of abusive and nonabusive mothers were shown videotapes of both crying and smiling infants. The abusers showed more intense physiological reactions to the crying infant, greater increases in blood pressure and heart rate, for instance, and they said they felt more annoyed than sympathetic toward the children pictured. Interestingly, the abusive mothers also reacted negatively to the movies of *smiling* children. They perceived the babies' smiles as demanding something (just as the cry demands attention), and the researchers concluded that the mothers felt they were unsuccessful at meeting any of their own children's needs.

The particular quality—the acoustics—of a baby's cry may put him at greater risk for abuse, according to recent research. Videotapes of premature infants, who have a typically high-pitched nonrhythmic cry, as well as "difficult" babies, whose cries are endless and shrill, have been shown to evoke particularly strong responses of aversion from viewers.

Of course, it's entirely normal to feel angry at your baby when she's out of control and you're overly tired and frustrated. Just because you get mad at her sometimes doesn't mean you're a potential abuser. Many factors—besides the infant's cries—play into child battering, including serious family situations such as marital discord, shaky finances, isolation of the mother, and a history of abuse in the parent's own background.

Viewing crying in a positive light: As the parent of a colicky baby, you're apt to feel disheartened much of the time. Coping with relentless crying is an uphill battle, but it's important that you don't let yourself give in to your feelings of hopelessness, or what psychologists call "learned helplessness." Some parents of nonstop screamers feel so out of control, they can't see the light at the end of the tunnel. They try every conceivable method to soothe their unhappy baby, and when nothing works, the parent thinks, "Well, all my attempts are futile, so I may just as well give up!" What's worse, a severely colicky baby, the one who's so wound up during his waking times that he can't give you the smiles you naturally crave, or cuddle lovingly in your arms, can leave you feeling as though you and your baby aren't responding to each other in a "normal" way.

After a period of weeks or months of trying to interact with a nonresponsive infant—and struggling in vain to comfort him—a parent can talk herself into believing that "nothing will help," and she may let the baby cry his lungs out, or she might tend to his needs but turn off her emotions. She feels she's failed one too many times, and she's not going to set herself up for another failure or rejection by her baby. (A parent who falls into the "learned helplessness" trap runs some risk of experiencing similar helplessness in the future, when she's trying to discipline a stubborn two-year-old or reason with a self-determined preschooler, for instance.)

When you feel that you can't possibly deal with your baby's sobs one minute longer, try to focus on that light at the end of the tunnel. Keep reminding yourself that your baby's colic will last three or four months and then it *will end*. After that, your baby will begin to respond to you with more frequent smiles as well as loving coos, and when she does cry, your efforts to comfort her will be much more effective.

It's also helpful to view your child's cries in the most positive light possible. Tell yourself that his whimpers are his language, the only real way he has at this point in his life of communicating his basic needs to you; remind yourself that he's not trying to manipulate you or reproach you in any way. If you respond to your baby as though he's speaking to you, rather than crying at you, you'll be well on your way to setting the foundation for a strong parent/child relationship.

And when you can't understand the messages your baby's trying to send you? Simply responding to him, letting your child know you're there and *want* to comfort him, is important. If you do that, you can rest assured that you're caring for your baby in the best way you—or any of us—know how.

2. Does Your Baby Have Colic?

"Doctor, my twelve-day-old daughter has been crying on and off all day long for the past few days. Do you think this is normal—or could she be colicky?" That's a question pediatricians and their nurses hear countless times from worried parents who aren't certain whether their baby is just normally fretful or is suffering from that mysterious "malady" parents dread—colic.

Colic has become a catchall term used to describe any seizure of hard, inconsolable crying that can't be linked to a discernible cause, and sometimes fussy babies are misdiagnosed as having colic while truly colicky infants may be regarded as difficult or temperamental. The word *colic* is derived from the Greek *Kōlon* and literally means "an acute, sharp pain in the abdomen." The first pediatric textbook, *The Boke of Chyldren*, published in 1553, referred to "colicke" as a "rumbling in the gut," and for centuries the theory persisted that a colicky baby's heartrending screams were triggered by severe gastric pain. Though researchers now feel the condition is linked to an immaturity of the central nervous system—rather than gastrointestinal problems—we still have a great deal to learn about colic.

What we do know for certain is that colic is not a disease or illness, that is, it's not caused by germs or bacteria or a serious congenital defect. And although a colicky baby may act as though he's sick (one mother says, "I was sure my son was going to die!"), colicky infants are perfectly normal and healthy in every respect. They're alert, eat ravenously, and gain weight steadily.

Colic is a condition, or set of symptoms, that begins in the first few weeks of life. Most cases emerge within five to ten days after a baby's birth, with some parents reporting onset as early as the first or second day. Affecting as many as 20 to 30 percent of all babies, colic typically lasts three months (hence, the phrase "three month colic" and the Chinese version, "hundred days crying"), though some babies experience colicky spells for as little as a few weeks, while in others the condition rages full force for four to six months. When a baby remains colicky past the sixth month or when symptoms appear suddenly after three months, doctors begin to suspect food allergy as the culprit.

Your doctor's dilemma: Diagnosing colic can be tricky since there is no "colic test." Babies aren't routinely X-rayed, nor do they undergo blood tests when their parents or pediatricians suspect colic, and even if they were X-rayed or their blood were analyzed, absolutely nothing indicating colic would show up. What's more, as we've seen, colicky crying mimics intense normal/fussy crying since both tend to last twelve weeks, then end suddenly or taper off gradually. Fussy babies cry as much as three hours a day and colicky babies regularly cry for three or more hours per day (some weary parents have reported that their babies have cried for up to twelve hours!). And both colicky and noncolicky babies often cry the longest and hardest during the afternoon and evening hours.

Because your pediatrician doesn't live with your child twenty-four hours a day, he's at a particular disadvantage when it comes to observing actual colicky symptoms. Most often, a doctor sees a baby during the "noncolicky hours," from 9:00 A.M. to 3:30 P.M., for instance; of course, many babies do cry during the day, but a rhythmical car ride to the doctor's office will often soothe the baby enough that she may not show a single colicky symptom when she's in the examining room. Many of us have had the frustrating experience of arriving at the doctor's office only to have our baby turn on the charm, smiling contentedly at the doctor as he pokes and prods. Then, as soon as we get her home and settled into her crib and begin to prepare dinner, she launches into a tirade we'd pay any price to have the doctor witness. It's understandable, then, that pediatricians sometimes mistakenly assume the parents are exaggerating when we describe the nightmare the family is going through, or that they tell us our baby is a little fussy and advise us not to get excited or upset!

Of course, a baby who cries excessively should be

examined thoroughly by a pediatrician, since certain illnesses mimic colic. Urinary-tract infections are often mistaken for colic, because the infant characteristically draws his legs up to his belly and screams in pain. Your doctor will need to catch a clean sample of urine (not an easy task with a tiny infant) and he may have to analyze two or three specimens before making an accurate diagnosis. A urinary-tract infection can be cleared up with antibiotics, but left undetected and untreated, it can cause kidney damage. An infant with an ear infection will also cry inconsolably and may draw his legs up in a tight fetal position (actually, a baby in any kind of pain will tend to pull his legs up to his stomach; watch for this reflex the next time your baby gets a shot). Like urinary-tract infections, ear infections require prompt treatment.

Occasionally, parents may assume their baby has colic when the baby is suffering from a rare, but potentially fatal, condition called pyloric stenosis, in which the opening of the stomach valve is smaller than usual and partially digested food can't pass through into the intestine. The most common symptom is projectile vomiting, though the baby will also cry long and hard and show signs of acute abdominal pain. Surgery is often required to correct this serious condition.

Once your doctor has ruled out an underlying medical problem as the cause of your baby's crying, the only way she can make a definite diagnosis is by considering your detailed description of the baby's symptoms.

Is there a colicky baby "type"?: Pediatrician T. Berry Brazelton has suggested that colicky babies do have a certain "personality," at least during the colicky phase. They're more restless and tense than other babies, more sensitive to external and internal stimulation. And they have a characteristic body language.

Most experts agree that colicky infants share the following symptoms or behavior:

1. *Excessive crying:* "Susan cried for what seemed like twenty-four hours a day," says Angela. "All I know is that my husband and I were always exhausted because we didn't get any sleep; her screaming went on round the clock."

There are degrees of colic, and some babies cry harder and longer than others. Angela's baby had severe colic and her crying was episodic and unpredictable over a twenty-four-hour period. Other babies have a regular pattern to their crying spells. "Nancy cried between 3:00 P.M. and 6:00 P.M. and then from 9:00 P.M. to 1:00 A.M.," says Bob, "so we were able to anticipate the rough times and try to get some rest when she was sleeping."

Still other babies are relatively calm all day long, crying "normally" when they need a diaper change or feel hungry, then they suddenly go into a crying jag around dinnertime. And while certain colicky babies cry every day without fail, others cry every other day —or even every third day.

What all these babies have in common, though, is that they cry for at least three hours for three or more days a week, and they're what doctors call "inconsolable." That is, they aren't able to soothe themselves, and their parents' attempts to calm them are often unsuccessful for more than a few minutes at a time (some experts feel that the "fussy" baby, in contrast, is more apt to be consoled when a parent picks him up or feeds him).

Parents also report that the quality of the colicky cry is different from noncolicky crying. There's a definite high-pitched or shrill, piercing characteristic to the colicky scream and, as Angela says, "It can be relentless, almost frantic like a plea."

Alice, who's the mother of two-and-a-half-month-old twins—one with colic, one without—says the cries of her two babies are very dissimilar. "Gary doesn't have colic and he cries only when he's hungry," explains Alice. "His cries are attention seeking, low-pitched, and whiny. Marissa's cries have a pitiful, high-pitched sound. There's a distinct difference between the two babies' cries, and Marissa's are much more disturbing."

2. *Extreme sensitivity:* Colicky infants tend to be sensitive to the slightest touch or sound, and even a tiny beam of light shining through the blinds in their nursery can waken them in an instant.

"Susan was good as gold her first day in the hospital," says Angela, "but on the second day, when my husband was holding her in his lap and sneezed suddenly, she practically jumped out of her blanket. After that, she was startled by everything. A little noise or a flicker of light could set her off on a screaming tangent."

All babies are born with a "startle reflex." A sudden loud noise or loss of equilibrium will cause them to stiffen, arch their backs, and thrust their arms and legs outward, then pull them inward as if clutching something and trying to regain their balance. But some experts have suggested that colicky babies have an overactive startle reflex that's easily set off by the tiniest noise, touch, or light. Maria describes her infant son as being "in constant startle position. It was terrible. He was a very light sleeper and I got really nervous and tense during his nap and bedtimes, making sure the TV was turned down low and that our daughter, Amy, was absolutely quiet. I think I could literally have dropped a pin outside his nursery door and he would have woken up!

"Finally, my mother and I took turns sitting with him in the nursery with all the shades pulled. We'd rock him for hours until he fell asleep. You can imagine what kind of life my family had during those months. Sitting in a dark room for much of the day was extremely draining on me, and my daughter's life was disrupted by her brother's condition. She couldn't invite her friends over to play and she had to keep her voice down whenever the baby was sleeping—and even when he was awake, since she didn't want to startle him into a screaming fit!"

When it comes to reacting to stimulation, there are actually two types of colicky babies. Both are extremely sensitive to external and internal stimulation (a colicky infant can become agitated by the sound of his own rumbling stomach or overly distressed by a gas bubble another baby might ignore completely), but one colicky infant needs to shut out all stimulation while the other requires *extra* stimulation from his parents to help distract him from his discomfort.

The first baby wants to tune out everything in his environment and become a little hermit during colicky spells, and his parents, like Maria, may spend many an hour sitting in a quiet, darkened nursery trying to get their infant to fall asleep. This type of baby may be soothed by very gentle rocking or soft music playing in the background, but he can't take too much of any kind of stimulation. One mother says, "My daughter was so sensitive to touch, she couldn't tolerate much handling," and while a light massage may work wonders on some colicky infants, this type of baby would probably begin to writhe and struggle if she were massaged.

The other baby needs to be the center of attention, in a sense. He does best when his parents distract him by carrying him, playing rhythmic music (he just may adore rock 'n' roll), taking him for a car ride, or swinging him back and forth, high and low (carefully cradled, of course!). One mother says of her son, "He was happiest at parties, surrounded by a roomful of noisy people. We'd put him in his infant seat and he'd hold court. The sights and sounds actually seemed to make him forget how miserable he'd felt a few minutes before."

Discovering the right method for calming your baby will take time and practice, but over the days and weeks, you'll tune in to the cues he's sending you.

3. *Colicky body language:* Watching an infant go through a colicky episode can be downright frightening to parents. The babies cry with their entire bodies, and the way they hold themselves, the contortions they manage, look like an exaggeration of a noncolicky baby's body movements.

"Susan would draw her legs up to her belly," says Angela. "She'd clench her fists and wave her arms angrily. At other times, she'd go rigid, thrusting her arms and legs straight out, her back arched, and just hold that position. That was the scariest thing to see. It looked so unnatural; you always think of babies curled up in their cribs or nestled against you. When she went rigid, it looked like her last attempt for help."

"Mark drew his legs up very tightly to his abdomen," says Maria. "He was so tense. Then he'd arch his back and go rigid, his arms and legs sticking straight out. I was honestly afraid he might break if I held him.

"For the first three months, my husband was too frightened to hold the baby much; I think Peter was afraid Mark would break, too. He would just creep past the nursery, peek in helplessly, then hurry off to take care of something around the house. We didn't bond with Mark as quickly as we did with our daughter—you just couldn't hold him or cuddle him long enough to feel that special closeness. I guess we really missed having a baby who responded to us, rather than trying to escape from our grasp."

4. *The appearance of abdominal pain:* Most parents of colicky babies say their infants appear to be experiencing severe gastric pain much of the time, especially during or after feedings. "My daughter would begin to suck greedily," says one mother, "but after a minute or two, she'd draw her legs up to her belly, then arch her back and scream." Other babies will eat heartily, but as soon as the feeding is over, they become distraught.

Carol says of her son, Michael, "His stomach would balloon out during a feeding. I've never seen anything like it!" Most colicky babies do have distended, hard bellies during or after eating and they may or may not pass gas.

Symptoms that aren't related to colic: As the parents of a baby you suspect has colic, you've probably been bombarded with a hodgepodge of misinformation about your baby's condition. A concerned aunt may tell you that spitting up frequently during a feeding is "normal" for a colicky infant. The nurse who lives down the block might tell you to expect your baby to be constipated most of the time, that colicky babies are prone to infrequent bowel movements. When you attempt to determine whether your baby has colic, it will help to weed out—and put to rest—some of the false notions that persist from generation to generation.

Although colicky babies, like noncolicky infants, can experience the following symptoms, none are related to colic: frequent spitting up during and after feedings; projectile vomiting; increased constipation or diarrhea; rashes, eczema, or wheezing. If your baby has any of these symptoms, you should bring them to your doctor's attention immediately.

3. Talking to Your Pediatrician

"My baby's doctor treated me like a hysterical woman, a hypochondriac," says Tony. "I described to him over and over how Nicholas screamed relentlessly, how we had to keep him in his carriage in a dark room or rock him constantly. How he'd double up in pain after eating.

"All the doctor would say is, 'Nick's just unusually fretful. Don't worry yourself, don't get so upset and tense, or you'll make him more tense!' The doctor wouldn't even diagnose colic. I think he took the approach that if he gave a 'name' to what Nicholas had, or made a diagnosis, I'd react even more strongly!"

When they've ruled out any serious illnesses and pinpointed definite colicky symptoms, most doctors, unlike Tony's pediatrician, will tell parents that their baby is indeed colicky (a few do refuse to put a label on the baby's symptoms, thinking—as Tony suspected —the parent will become even more agitated). But many, like Tony's doctor, will also try to reassure parents by telling them not to worry, that their baby isn't suffering from "anything serious," and if the doctor is brusque, if he tries to hurry the parent out of his office or ends a phone call abruptly, his words can come off as sounding patronizing and unconcerned. Often, a doctor, especially one who's never had to cope with a colicky child him- or herself, doesn't realize how stressed parents can become, and how easy it is when a child cries constantly to imagine the worst. As Tony says, "I found myself thinking Nicholas might have some dread disease like cystic fibrosis and that the doctor had incorrectly diagnosed him as 'fretful.' When you're with a screaming baby twenty-four hours a day, one who looks like he's in the severest pain, your imagination *can* run wild."

Granted, most pediatricians are very busy people; they see dozens of babies every day, and many don't have the time or patience to deal with what they see as a simple case of colic, a condition that is self-limiting and can't possibly harm the baby. But they should make time to talk with you, to reassure you in a sincere manner that your baby is healthy and normal in every way, and to offer support.

A caring, concerned doctor will either take your calls or try to get back to you as soon as possible when your baby is experiencing a particularly violent colic attack and you feel as though you desperately need some professional advice or reassurance. "Susan's doctor was great," says Angela. "My husband and I kept telling each other, 'Something must be horribly wrong with our baby. Intellectually we knew she had colic and we trusted our doctor's diagnosis, but when we listened to her frantic screams, the mere word *colic* just didn't seem to realistically describe her condition.

"We felt we could call on her pediatrician anytime, and she would give us positive reinforcement. She'd sympathize with us, saying we were going through a horrible, rough time, but to try not to worry about Susan. She reminded us that Susan was healthy as a horse, eating normally and gaining weight steadily, and she emphasized that there *would* be an end to this whole, miserable time.

"Even though the doctor couldn't be there with us, walking Susan and comforting her, the sympathetic reassurances went a long way in giving us the strength we needed to carry on."

Angela's pediatrician is the ideal; she reassures parents that their baby won't be harmed by the colic, but she offers a sympathetic ear as well. If you feel your pediatrician isn't meeting your needs—or those of your child—if he seems condescending or refuses to answer all your questions about colic, if he tells you the problem is minor—"It's just gas!"—or if he doesn't examine your baby thoroughly to rule out any underlying medical conditions, such as urinary-tract or ear infections, change doctors! Many times we're hesitant to switch to a new pediatrician; after all, the doctor we're seeing is an expert, right? And when a doctor is patronizing, we can even begin to wonder if we are, actually, hysterical parents who imagine the worst when our baby doubles up in pain. But keep in mind that you have rights and so does your baby. Just as you may have "shopped around" for a pediatrician before your baby was born (an increasingly common practice), you may have to change doctors now in order to get the support you need during your baby's colicky period.

In order to help your doctor make an accurate diagnosis of colic, as well as establish a good rapport with her, it's important to be as thorough as possible when you describe your baby's symptoms—and to be up front about the effect your child's condition is having on you and your family. (If you're feeling overwhelmed, this is no time to maintain a brave, stiff-upper-lip facade.)

1. It's a good idea to write down in detail all the symptoms your baby is experiencing (review the four "colic behaviors" described in chapter 2, noting which ones apply to your baby).

2. Keep a crying diary or chart, noting the times of day your baby cries and the duration. Whenever possible, isolate a cause—e.g., wetness, hunger—but be sure to mention unexplained cry times as well. If there's a pattern to your baby's cries, if she wails at regular times during the day, chart this also.

3. Bring any unusual symptoms, such as constipation, diarrhea, vomiting, frequent spitting up, to the doctor's attention.

4. If you're breast-feeding, tell your doctor about your diet; he may want you to eliminate certain foods to rule out food allergy or determine whether a particular food that's passed through your breast milk, such as onions or garlic, is causing colicky symptoms.

5. If your baby is bottle-fed, tell the doctor which type of formula the child is taking and whether it contains iron; some infants are unable to tolerate iron supplements during the first few months and have extreme colicky reactions when taking an iron-fortified formula.

6. If your doctor initially dismisses your layman's diagnosis of colic, make a tape recording of your baby's cries at their worst and let the doctor listen to the sound and quality of your baby's wails. Some doctors will ask for tape recordings of a baby's cries—especially in the case of the baby who screams only at night and is content when she sees the doctor during the day. By listening to a recording, the pediatrician can distinguish between your baby's colicky cries and those of hunger or boredom.

7. Tell your doctor that you're feeling fatigued and helpless; and if there are any extenuating circumstances that make this a particularly difficult time for you (marital or financial problems, for instance) or if you feel increasingly hostile toward your child, share these concerns with the doctor. He may give you additional support by calling every few days to ask how you're coping, or he may suggest that you talk to a

clergyperson or counselor to relieve some of the pressure you're under.

It's wise to remember that even the best pediatrician won't have all the answers about infant colic—or your baby's colic in particular. What's more, your doctor is used to isolating an illness or problem and "curing" it, so she may feel as frustrated and helpless as you do in alleviating your baby's symptoms. She doesn't know your child in the same intimate way you do, and it's unlikely that she'll be able to tell you which method— or methods—will work best in calming your child. Here, you, rather than your doctor, are the expert, and you'll need to test various "remedies" through a trial-and-error approach (in chapter 5, we'll discuss the many "colic-calmers" that parents, like you, have found to be effective).

But if your doctor examines your baby thoroughly to rule out a serious medical problem, and if she offers a friendly, sympathetic ear, showing that she sincerely cares about both you and your baby, she can do a great deal to help you through this tough time.

4. What Causes Colic?

"It's just a little case of colic," says your well-meaning pediatrician, "gas pockets in Annie's belly. We'll try her on a soy formula for a week and see if that doesn't do the trick!"

"Nonsense," asserts your aunt (who's raised four noncolicky children and is incredibly—and annoyingly—calm when it comes to taking care of babies). "There's absolutely nothing wrong with Annie—nothing that can't be cured with a little tender loving care, that is. All you need to do is *relax* and the baby will relax. You're passing *your* tension on to *her!*"

"I've seen this type of baby before," your sister assures you. "Don't blame yourself. Annie's definitely a difficult child, fretful and peevish. *It's her temperament.* Brace yourself: she'll probably be this way for the next eighteen years!"

"Are you eating anything that might be making your milk go 'bad'?" asks your mother. "I remember whenever I ate spaghetti sauce, *you* were up all night wailing. We think you were allergic to tomatoes!"

Everyone—from your next-door neighbor to the mailman—will speculate as to the cause of your child's incessant crying, and by now you've probably been inundated with various "theories" about the cause (or causes) of colic. Actually no one, not even the top pediatric researchers, knows for certain what causes this baffling condition, though many theories have been suggested over the years.

There's a dearth of sound medical information about infant colic. Most major studies were conducted before the mid-1960's and few in-depth follow-ups have been done since, perhaps because colic isn't one of the more glamorous areas of study: it's a self-limiting, short-lived condition that causes no real harm to the baby, and so, most top researchers would rather spend their time searching for the causes and cures of the more life-threatening childhood diseases (let's face it, no one will ever win a Nobel Prize for colic research!). Add to this the fact that the medical community is somewhat uneasy about this mystery condition. As mentioned in chapter 2, there's no "colic test"; evidence of the condition can't be isolated on X rays or in blood tests. And since no animals exhibit colicky symptoms, animal research is pointless.

Most studies have been based on observation of groups of colicky and noncolicky babies in an attempt to determine which behaviors or symptoms the colicky infants share. Some researchers have asked parents to take part in the studies, keeping diaries that record the length and frequency of crying spells as well as any unusual behaviors. But in these cases the studies are naturally biased since parents of colicky infants are under extreme stress and their observations aren't always objective or even accurate.

While some of the early colic studies were done on large groups of children (more than one hundred), others focused on small numbers of babies (seven or eight) and the researchers pointed out that their samples were too small to make any definite conclusions. In addition, since colic lasts such a short time, usually three or four months, long-term studies are impossible. And finally, because the patient is a baby and can't describe his symptoms, we can only *assume* certain things: Does the baby feel pain? If so, where? Or is he merely emotionally strung out? Is he experiencing both pain and stress—and if that's the case, which comes first? Does one trigger the other? No one can say for certain.

It *will* help to take a look at the major theories about colic—from the belief that it is precipitated by a gastrointestinal disorder to the idea that maternal anxiety is the culprit—since pediatricians still vary widely in their own notions about the condition and it's not unlikely that your doctor may ascribe to one (or more) of the outdated theories.

Gastrointestinal difficulties: The theory that colic is caused by a gastrointestinal disorder is firmly entrenched, and friends, relatives—even your child's doctor—may assure you that your baby merely has stomach problems, anything from pent-up gas to painful "kinking" or spasms in the digestive tract. Even the term *colic* is derived from the word *colon* and literally means "a sharp pain in the gut." And, too, colicky infants certainly seem to be experiencing severe gastric discomfort: because the baby characteristically draws his legs up to his tummy and has a hard, distended abdomen, parents and pediatricians alike logically assume the infant's trouble "lies in the belly."

As Alice points out, "My daughter's pediatrician was very pragmatic. He told me the baby had gas bubbles she couldn't pass and he felt the formula I was giving her might be causing the problem. He suggested I switch to a soy formula, but that didn't help. Then he decided Marissa's digestive system was 'immature' and couldn't digest food properly."

Another mother, Arlene, remembers, "The doctor felt Tamara had gas. He gave me a medication, some sort of 'colic drops,' to break up the gas bubbles, but it didn't work. I still think the colic must have had something to do with her stomach, though, since she demanded to nurse all the time. It was as if she had to keep her stomach full in order to feel okay. She'd nurse, fall asleep for five minutes, then wake up screaming and want to nurse again!"

Overfeeding, underfeeding, and the excessive and "trapped gas" theories: For decades, pediatricians suspected that over- or under-feeding caused colic attacks in infants; either the hungry baby wasn't getting enough food and acids accumulated in his empty stomach (causing gassiness and cramping) or he was getting too much food and "bloating up." Other pediatricians felt that colicky babies were merely prone to excessive gas, or that due to some spasm or temporary kinking in the lower loops of the bowel, they couldn't get rid of pent-up gas.

No studies show conclusively that the number of times an infant eats or the amount of food he consumes has anything to do with colic attacks. Colicky babies seem to gain weight steadily, and perhaps even faster, than noncolicky infants, and their typical need to "nurse" more frequently may be linked to the soothing nature of sucking itself. But some doctors still caution parents to keep their colicky babies on a strict feeding schedule (nursing or bottle-feeding every two-and-a-half to three hours rather than every fifteen to forty-five minutes, which many colicky babies seem to demand). They suggest that when the baby "roots" for his mother's breast between feedings, the parents give him a little sugar water or lukewarm water in a bottle.

R. S. Illingworth, one of the most prominent researchers in the colic field (and Britain's answer to Dr. Spock!), X-rayed seven colicky infants in 1954 to determine whether excessive gas was causing their discomfort. He also X-rayed seven noncolicky babies and then asked a radiologist to grade the X rays according to the amount of gas in each infant's digestive tracts.

Although Illingworth admitted that seven babies comprised too small a sample to draw any definite conclusions, the results were interesting—and surprising. Five of the seven colicky infants had normal intestinal gas, while two colicky babies and three noncolicky infants showed only a slight increase in the amount of gas. None of the colicky babies—but three of the noncolicky infants—showed large amounts of gas!

Based on this and other studies, Illingworth speculated that colicky infants aren't prone to *excessive* gas, but they may suffer from gas trapped in the lower bowel, due to some unexplained spasm or kinking in the intestine. In this instance, a baby may produce a "normal" amount of gas during and after feedings, but he can't pass it and his belly becomes painfully bloated.

Today, many researchers and pediatricians feel that gas does play a role in colic, but the question is, does gas *cause* colic or is it merely a consequence of colic? Most likely, gassiness is caused by the colic itself. As many doctors point out, a baby in the throes of a violent crying spell gulps large quantities of air that must be expelled in some manner. This air can get trapped in the intestinal tract and make the baby feel even more miserable than he did at the outset of his crying jag.

Contractions in the digestive tract: In 1952, another noted colic researcher, Sweden's Dr. S. Jorup, X-rayed babies in an attempt to find a gastrointestinal cause for colic. Like Illingworth, Jorup found that colicky infants showed no increased intestinal gas, but he did link colic attacks to motility problems, or the way foodstuffs pass through the intestines. The X rays showed that as the food moved around the large S-shaped sigmoid colon, which empties into the rectum, the babies' colons contracted violently—and at that moment the babies would stop nursing and pull their legs up to their bellies. If the colon muscles remained contracted, the babies were fussy and irritable during the entire feeding. (For years, pediatricians prescribed antispasmodics to relieve these painful abdominal contractions, but today fewer doctors use these powerful medications to treat colic since they can have serious side effects. More about drug therapy will be discussed in chapter 6.)

An immature digestive system: More recently, researchers have moved toward the theory that colic is caused by an immature digestive system. This hypothesis seems logical: after all, during the early months of your baby's life, all her systems are somewhat disorganized. Her heart rate and breathing aren't yet regulated, and it's possible that in some babies, the stomach and intestines just aren't working smoothly. Food may not move easily through the intestines; spasms may occur for some unknown reason; the digestive system may not produce the enzymes needed to break down certain carbohydrates and fats in breast milk or formula. An even more intriguing theory links possible gastrointestinal problems to the baby's immature central nervous system (we'll talk in more depth about central nervous system changes later on). It's conceivable that the colicky infant's central nervous system is sending faulty messages to the digestive tract, causing painful spasms or contractions in the bowels.

Diet (mother's and baby's): The role of diet in colic has been debated for decades. Many pediatricians still feel that switching formulas is the best method of managing colic in bottle-fed babies. Indeed, a recent article in a leading pediatrics journal associates an allergy to cow's milk with colic, pointing out that there may be a *subgroup* of colicky babies (possibly 30 to 35 percent!) who have an increased sensitivity to cow's-milk products, and that their symptoms are lessened or relieved entirely when milk products are eliminated from their diet.

Studies show that some babies are lactose-intolerant, that is, they aren't able to digest the lactose or milk sugars found in cow's milk—either in formula or in breast milk (mothers who consume dairy products can pass the elements in cow's milk on to their nursing babies). If the infant is being breast-fed, the mother may be asked to limit or eliminate dairy products from her diet, under her doctor's supervision, to make sure both she and her baby receive proper nutrition. If the infant is being bottle-fed, the pediatrician may switch her to a soy-based formula, but that isn't always the answer. Rather than being lactose-intolerant, the baby may be unable to digest milk *protein*, and cow's-milk protein and soy protein are alike in structure. In this case, an elemental—or predigested—formula is the best prescription (elemental formulas are costly, almost double the price of regular formula). Switching and testing various formulas takes time and patience, but the right formula can relieve colicky symptoms in *some* babies. If after two weeks, though, a baby is still cranky and distressed, her diet probably isn't causing the colicky symptoms.

There's some evidence that foods other than dairy products in a mother's diet can precipitate colicky symptoms in nursing babies. Even noncolicky infants are often sensitive—and experience gassiness, cramping, and crying spells—when their moms eat certain foods. Says Anne, "Daniel wasn't colicky, but every time I ate garlic or onions during his first three months, he was miserable. Irritable, crying—and passing a lot of gas."

Foods that have been connected to colicky symptoms in breast-fed babies include: chocolate, eggs, citrus fruits, nuts, garlic, onions, broccoli, cabbage, wheat, oats, shellfish, corn, and green peppers. Also, caffeine has been shown to make babies irritable as well as gassy, and it's best to limit caffeine intake (or cut it out entirely) while you're breast-feeding. Coffee, tea, some carbonated soft drinks, and chocolate contain caffeine.

If you feel your diet may be playing a role in your baby's discomfort, eliminate the "suspect" foods from your diet one at a time (do this under your doctor's supervision). Stop eating a certain food for a week and observe your baby to see if her colicky spells decrease in frequency or intensity. If nothing happens, eliminate the next food on your list for one week and so on.

Maternal anxiety: The notion that maternal anxiety or tension can trigger or exacerbate colic has been one of the most hotly debated issues in colic research! And although the newest studies have almost conclusively proven that maternal tensions—before or after the baby's birth—have little or no effect on the infant's condition, some pediatricians will still tell an understandably anxious mother that she's passing her own tensions on to her child. As one mother put it, "The doctor treated me like a hypochondriac, as though the baby's condition was all in my head. He implied that when *I* calmed down, my son would, too!"

The idea that a mother can somehow condition her baby to be cranky and temperamental persists, and many moms even harbor guilt feelings about their possible role in their baby's colic. "I was very tense during my pregnancy," says Laura. "I'd had one miscarriage, and when I was pregnant with Margie, I stained throughout the first three months. I was terribly afraid something might be wrong.

"Then, right after I gave birth, I became totally overwhelmed, crying uncontrollably and feeling strung out (the doctor thinks I may have experienced a reaction to the three cervical blocks he gave me as well as a small dose of Demerol to help me with the pain). Every time the nurses brought Margie to me, I'd panic. I couldn't hold her—I just kept passing out, and although intellectually I feel as though I didn't cause Margie's colic, I sometimes wonder, 'But what if I did have something to do with it?'"

Another mother recalls that while she was quite

contented and calm during her first pregnancy and gave birth to a very calm baby, she and her husband were having marital problems when she was pregnant with the couple's second child. "I had very ambivalent feelings about having a second child," says Tess. "I was very happy, very fulfilled, with just one child, but my husband wanted at least two kids. We waited until our first son was five before we tried to have another baby. I felt anxious during the entire pregnancy, perhaps because of the difficulties Matt and I were having, possibly because I wasn't ready to have a second baby. When Thomas turned out to be colicky, I refused to lay that guilt trip about the 'mother's mental state causing the child's colic' on myself. But from time to time, I find myself thinking maybe my emotions did have something to do with his condition."

From the 1950's on, various researchers have studied mothers of colicky infants to determine what, if any, role their emotions played in the babies' colicky behavior. Most studies required the mothers to answer detailed personality questionnaires regarding their emotions during and after pregnancy. A few studies indicated that mothers who were tense, depressed, anxious, or ambivalent about being pregnant were more apt to give birth to colicky infants. Other studies found that a mother's mental state during pregnancy had absolutely no connection with the incidence of colic. (Keep in mind, too, that many women who are depressed or anxious during pregnancy give birth to *non*colicky babies.)

Some studies suggested that overly anxious—or

even "neurotic," fearful—women passed their tensions on to their newborns, thus triggering colicky reactions. Now, it's entirely possible that a tense mother may pass *some* of her anxiety on to her infant; babies are remarkably perceptive little people and they can pick up on the emotions and moods of both their parents or other care-givers. But recent studies show that it's highly unlikely that maternal anxiety (or paternal tension, for that matter) can cause or even aggravate colic.

In 1974, researcher Benjamin A. Shaver compared mothers of colicky infants with those of noncolicky babies. Shaver pointed out that after twelve weeks, the mothers of the colicky infants *were* significantly less confident in their parenting skills than the other mothers. But by the time the babies were twenty-four weeks old (approximately two months after the colic had subsided in most cases), the mothers of the colicky babies had become more confident and there seemed to be no significant difference between the two groups of mothers.

Shaver's study is important because it points out that mothers who become tense and upset during their baby's colicky phase aren't necessarily unstable or neurotic. Any parent who must cope with an incessantly crying infant (and manage on a few hours of sleep to boot!) is likely to respond to a colicky baby with frustration, depression—and increased anxiety. But those feelings pass when the baby's colic passes. Most experts now feel that a baby's colic causes anxiety and frustration in the mother (and dad, too), not the reverse.

In defense of mothers, researchers also note that a colicky baby tends to act up even when he's being cared for by someone other than his mom. Says Maria, "My mother moved in with us and took care of my son. Mom is extremely patient and calm and she spent hours rocking and consoling the baby while he screamed. I don't think her calmness really had an effect on him—which made me realize my *tension* wasn't causing the problem. It's just that Mom's ability to stay calm herself helped *her* in the long run. She could spend that extra hour comforting the baby when I was emotionally and physically drained and ready to plop him in his crib!"

Experts also note that the majority of colicky babies aren't necessarily first-borns. Colic can occur just as frequently among second-, third-, or fourth-borns. A mother may give birth to two "normal," sweet-tempered infants, only to find that her third child is a screamer. It stands to reason that a first-time mother is the most anxious and most likely to question her parenting skills. So why, then, would she be any more tense with subsequent children?

Also, if maternal anxiety were the missing piece in the colic puzzle, then logically, a baby's colic should always emerge within the first few days of life when his mother is most anxious, and, justifiably, emotional. But that's not the case; many colic episodes begin five to ten days after the baby's birth—and sometimes even later.

Finally there's the intriguing situation of the premature baby. Understandably the mother of a premature infant is especially anxious, worrying about possible health problems and wondering when her baby can come home from the hospital. More than any other mother, she will question her ability to be a good parent to a baby who may be at risk. One would think, based on all this, that a premature baby would develop colicky symptoms within days (or even hours) after his birth. But that's not the case. Typically, the premature baby doesn't become colicky until several days or weeks after the mother's *due* date—the same time full-term babies develop colic!

If you're one of those unlucky mothers whose pediatrician has implied that your mental state during your pregnancy or your anxiety about your baby's condition (or, worse still, your feelings of inadequacy about your parenting skills!) is at the root of your baby's problem, you might want to consider changing pediatricians. It's important to remember that doctors often feel frustrated when dealing with colic cases; in an area where there are so many unknowns, where a physiological cause and cure can't be isolated, it's not uncommon for a few insensitive physicians to offhandedly remark that a baby's colic may be related to your psychological state. Even today, there are a number of male doctors who still regard women as "hysterical." And even some female pediatricians, who have never endured the trauma of caring for a colicky baby themselves, sometimes lay the blame at the mother's feet.

The most sensitive—and informed—doctors, however, are those who realize that the mother of a colicky infant has enough to deal with and doesn't need her child's pediatrician suggesting that she may be the cause of her baby's unhappiness. Blessedly, the "maternal anxiety" theory is slowly being laid to rest by the medical community.

Prenatal drugs and colic: There's considerable debate as to whether drugs taken during pregnancy or given to a mother during labor and delivery can make babies more prone to colic. Evidence does show that any substance found in the mother's blood that isn't altered or destroyed before passing through the placenta *can* be transferred to the baby. Even medications given to the mother to reduce pain during the last stages of delivery may affect the infant, and after the baby is born his immature system must break down and eliminate the drugs, a process that can take days or weeks.

In one recent study, a group of Australian researchers linked the use of the epidural (an anesthetic used during childbirth that numbs the lower half of the woman's body) to colic. Studying forty babies whose mothers had had epidurals, the team found that all of the babies were trembly, irritable, and had poorer body coordination than babies delivered without the use of drugs. The infants in the epidural group also cried more after the first week of birth, and by one month they were more tense, more difficult to manage —and less adaptable than other babies. Another study, using Brazelton's temperament analysis of newborns, indicated that babies of women who received general anesthesia during delivery were difficult up to one month of age, taking longer to calm down. These babies were also generally less cuddly and more easily startled than most babies.

More extensive research on the association between

prenatal drugs and colic is needed, but we must take into account that many women who have received medications during pregnancy and labor have given birth to noncolicky babies. And, conversely, mothers who have received no medication have borne colicky infants.

Complications during birth: Some studies also point to a possible link between colic and oxygen deprivation during birth. Researchers have found that infants who undergo prolonged, difficult labors and deliveries and suffer from an inadequate supply of oxygen during and after birth may be more prone to colicky behavior, including extreme irritability and a tendency to sleep less and waken often during the first few months of life.

Hormonal deficiency: One of the more intriguing hypotheses ties the incidence of colic to low progesterone levels in colicky babies.

During pregnancy, the placenta produces progesterone, a hormone that stimulates relaxation of the smooth muscles of the intestines—and may affect the central nervous system as well, having a calming and sleep-inducing effect on the infant. Newborns generally receive high levels of placental progesterone at birth, but after a few days (or, in some cases, one or two weeks), this progesterone wears off and the baby begins to produce the hormone herself.

A 1963 study showed that colicky infants have very low levels of progesterone compared to noncolicky babies, and once the infants were given a progesterone-like drug, their colic symptoms improved (of course, most doctors are reluctant to use hormones to treat a short-term condition like colic). More recent studies have linked low progesterone levels to colic, though other studies show no evidence of a connection. Proponents of the "progesterone/colic" theory note, however, that colic attacks typically begin at about the same time as a baby's placental progesterone starts to "wear off"—a few days to one or two weeks after she's born.

Does temperament play a role? Some researchers, including T. Berry Brazelton, have suggested that the colicky baby has a definite "personality type," an in-born temperament that makes him naturally more active and sensitive to stimulation than other babies. Dr. S. Jorup believed that colicky infants were more sensitive to sound and light, that they slept for shorter periods of time than other babies, that they seemed "restless" in general.

All babies are born with a certain temperament that can be measured as early as the first day after birth. And, typically, colicky babies do seem "difficult," often overly sensitive to the slightest stimulation. But the question remains: is the colicky baby's behavior the result of a "difficult" temperament, or is the difficult temperament a consequence of the colic itself, triggered by the pain or stress the baby is experiencing? No one can say for certain.

And while one prominent researcher attempted to tie long-term difficult temperament to colic (saying

that colicky babies were more likely to become difficult older infants and toddlers), other research and
common sense tells us this isn't the case. For instance,
many studies—and parents—report that colicky
babies are no more likely than noncolicky infants to
become hard-to-handle toddlers and children. In fact,
once a baby emerges from that colicky stage, he often,
almost miraculously, turns into an easygoing, normally
happy child. Says Tess, "One week Thomas was colicky, a terror, a kid I almost hated. The next week,
when the colic subsided, he became an absolute angel,
adorable, delightful—it was like day and night!"

Many parents point out, too, that their colicky
babies aren't difficult all the time, that when these
babies aren't fussing or screaming, they are absolutely
lovable—like miniature Jekyll and Hydes. "When
Marissa is quiet—which she generally is until late afternoon (the time her colic attacks start in earnest)—
she's luscious," says Alice. "You'd never know there
was anything wrong with her. She's affable, she smiles
and coos and is very loving." With such reports from
parents, it's tricky to pinpoint a definite "colic personality." Some babies, like Marissa, have their good
times and their bad times, while others are miserable
and testy twenty-four hours a day.

Perhaps the most logical explanation of these "temperament" changes is that colicky babies *are* extremely
sensitive, but not all the time. That's why their temperaments seem to change suddenly during the course of
a day. Researchers now feel that colic isn't linked
to temperament, but rather to changes in the central

nervous system that can mimic temperament problems.

The role of the central nervous system: Over the years, many researchers have suggested that an immaturity of the central nervous system (CNS) is the key to the mystery of colic. Even as early as 1901 (and through the 1940's) colicky babies were described as "hypertonic," or having exaggerated or rigid muscle tension caused by an "imbalance in the nervous system." More recently, colicky babies have been said to possess lower sensory thresholds—that is, they are easily startled—and distressed—by the slightest sounds, sights, even by a gentle touch.

But logically, we might ask, why does one newborn's nervous system seem to work perfectly well while another's isn't functioning smoothly? Actually all babies are born with "immature" nervous systems, but the maturity level may vary considerably from one newborn to the next. Babies aren't necessarily all the "same age" when they're born. The mother's due date is, at best, an estimate, and few babies arrive on the day they are expected. Most, in fact, are born within two weeks before or after the due date. Also, one baby's rate of development before birth can be faster than another's. The easygoing, placid baby may come into the world "prepared" to handle the sights and sounds, the stimulation that surrounds her. Although, technically, her central nervous system is immature—that is, it will need to settle into place over the next few months—she has a head start because her CNS is *less* immature than that of the colicky baby. As a result, she has a better grasp on her motor and coping skills; she's able to find and suck on her thumb or fingers when she's distressed. She's also more easily calmed by care-givers because she's just naturally less wound up than the colicky baby. Her brain is sending appropriate messages to the various parts of her body and her digestive system is working smoothly, her arms and legs are becoming increasingly coordinated, and she has some control over them.

The colicky infant, on the other hand, is most likely born with a less-developed central nervous system. Her brain may send "faulty" messages to her gastrointestinal tract, causing the muscles to work unevenly, and it's possible that she's experiencing painful spasms during or after feedings. Her other systems may be receiving inappropriate messages from the brain as well. Remember that the central nervous system controls the brain, the spinal cord—and all the nerves originating therefrom. An immature CNS may trigger spasms or reactions in any of the nerves or muscles, those in the arms, legs, neck—and this may explain why colicky babies often seem out of control, as though something has gone haywire in their systems. So many mothers describe their infants as appearing "unnatural at times," totally rigid, with arms and legs suddenly sticking straight out, then flailing around as though the infant were trying desperately to "grab" on to something or restore his sense of equilibrium. These attacks happen suddenly; they can come out of nowhere. A baby who has been content for the past hour can suddenly become "unglued" and "wired," as one mother put it. It's as though his brain mistakenly sent a message to his limbs, saying "swing around wildly!" while he has absolutely no control over what's happening.

And, too, the theory that colicky babies possess an incredibly low sensory threshold can be explained by CNS immaturity. Whereas the easygoing baby often isn't fazed by internal or external stimuli, the colicky child can go crazy at the mere sound of her own growling stomach or a parent's sneeze. It would seem that her nervous system is capable of handling only so much stimulation during those first few months—until it begins to function smoothly, sending proper signals to the various parts of her body.

Interestingly, colic researchers have come full circle during this century. The German pediatrician who associated colic with "hypertonia" or an imbalance in the nervous system in 1901 actually predicted our current thinking about colic, that it is, in all likelihood, related to CNS immaturity. And some researchers have gone so far as to suggest that the unexplained crying of colic may be just that—inexplicable in that the crying infant may not be trying to communicate *any specific need* to her parents. These scientists feel it's possible that colicky screaming is merely an indication that the central nervous system is disorganized and overwhelmed, and when frustrated parents say, "I don't understand what he wants—he just cries and cries," they may be absolutely on target. The baby may be crying for "no good reason," other than that her system has just gone haywire for a time!

As parents, it's only natural that we may feel concerned when we hear our colicky baby has an "immature" nervous system, that he's slower to adapt to the pressures of the world around him. One mother asked, "If my child has something wrong with her nervous system, does that mean she won't be as smart or quick to catch on to things as other kids?"

Testimony from thousands of parents of colicky children supports experts' belief that once the colicky phase passes, a child learns as quickly as other infants his age. Recent studies also suggest that colicky or "difficult" infants may actually develop superior cognitive and social skills than their noncolicky counterparts—perhaps because their parents interacted with them so much during early infancy. (For more information about this subject, see chapter 8.)

Drawing some conclusions: Although no one can say for certain what causes some babies to become colicky, experts now feel the condition is triggered by multiple factors. A subgroup of colicky babies may be allergic or sensitive to the elements in cow's milk, and these infants require special diets. In other babies, colic is most likely caused by an immaturity of the central nervous system, and as a result, an infant has difficulty handling both external and internal stimulation; he's also unable to inhibit his states of "arousal"—both feelings of distress or being out of control and the crying that inevitably occurs. Once he's launched into a crying jag, he doesn't possess the coping skills to calm himself.

Many experts also feel that gas does play a role in

colic, but the current feeling is that gassiness is a consequence rather than the cause of colic. And while painful spasms or contractions in the digestive tract may be a symptom of colic, it's likely that they're precipitated by messages the brain sends to the digestive system (CNS involvement).

Conditions that don't relate to colic: Over the years, researchers have attempted to link colic to any number of conditions or circumstances, but based on numerous studies, experts have ruled out some of the more common beliefs about the causes of colic. Colic has nothing to do with: the baby's sex; mother's weight gain during pregnancy; baby's weight gain after birth; incidence of nausea or morning sickness during mother's pregnancy; whether the baby is breast- or bottle-fed; incidence of spitting up, diarrhea, constipation, or convulsions in the baby; incidence of fetal hiccups; mother's or family's economic status; mother's level of education.

We'll talk about some of these—and other improbable—causes of colic in the next chapter, which discusses the more common myths about this baffling condition.

5. Myths About Colic

Because colic is a condition that puzzles pediatricians and parents alike, dozens of myths have evolved over the years, misinformation that has been passed along from generation to generation. Some of these notions are so firmly entrenched in our culture (for example, "Gas causes colic") that they begin to sound plausible to us, and separating fact from fiction can become a guessing game.

Here are some of the most common old wives' tales about colic.

1. *Firstborn babies are more prone to colic:* Research shows that firstborns are no more susceptible to colic than second-, third-, or fourth-born children. A mother may give birth to several noncolicky infants, then—out of the blue—bear a colicky baby. Birth order seems to have no correlation with colic.

2. *If your first baby was colicky, it's likely your next child will be colicky, too:* Although some studies indicate that a high ratio of colicky babies have older siblings who were afflicted with the condition during infancy, there's no definite proof that colic "runs in families." Also, many large families report having one colicky infant as well as several noncolicky babies.

3. *Boys are colicky more often than girls:* For decades, boys have been perceived as "more difficult," rambunctious, and harder to handle than girls, and perhaps that's what spawned the notion that boys are more apt to be colicky. Research has proven conclusively, however, that equal numbers of boys *and* girls tend to be colicky.

4. *Colic can occur anytime during baby's first year of life:* Although older infants sometimes exhibit coliclike symptoms (increased gassiness, intestinal cramping, and excessive crying), colic typically begins within the first few weeks after birth. When symptoms suddenly begin after three months, the baby may be suffering from an unrelated condition such as an ear infection, urinary-tract infection, or food allergy.

5. *Fetal hiccups in utero signal a predisposition to colic:* In a 1950 study that attempted to connect fetal hiccups to colic, a researcher reported that those babies who hiccuped frequently in utero were more likely to be allergic to cow's milk and have colicky

symptoms after birth. But later research shows no correlation between hiccups and colic.

6. *Certain races show a higher incidence of colic:* There's absolutely no relationship between race and colic, though some *cultures* are reported to have a lower incidence of the condition. In certain non-Western societies, where babies are carried most of the day by their mothers, colic is virtually unknown. But this is due to the infants' close proximity to the mother, not to genetic factors.

7. *You will spoil a colicky baby if you pick him up too often:* Many people still ascribe to the old belief (based on early behavioral studies) that a baby who receives too much attention will learn to "manipulate" his parents or become overly demanding. But numerous studies show that infants who are attended to and carried frequently during their first few months actually cry less than if they weren't comforted. And in later infancy, they tend to use noncrying forms of communication, such as gurgles and facial expressions, to signal their needs.

By picking up and comforting your baby when he cries, you teach him to trust—not manipulate—you.

8. *Colicky babies are apt to be "hyperactive" later on:* Because colicky babies appear so agitated, because they startle easily, sleep for short periods, and seem to be "wired" and excessively active, researchers naturally suspected these infants might be prone to hyper-

activity as they grew older. However, no studies have proven a link between colic and hyperactivity, and the restlessness colicky babies experience during their first tumultuous months usually disappears once the colic subsides.

9. *Colicky babies are calmer when someone other than their parents takes care of them:* This idea harkens back to the theory of maternal anxiety, but here the father's anxiety is also suspect. Sometimes, babies *do* seem to calm down more quickly when an aunt or grandmother or sitter cares for them, but it's possible that a third party, one who's not so emotionally involved with the infant's condition, is merely less tired than the parents and, therefore, willing and able to spend more time calming the baby. Whereas the father who's spent two hours consoling his infant may be exhausted once the episode is over, a grandmother who rocks the baby for two hours may often appear fresh and ready to tackle some other task around the house. We might think Grandma has calmed the baby more quickly (and effectively) when in reality she's merely outlasted him! A third party has more emotional and physical stamina than the wearied parents who must deal with a screaming baby twenty-four hours a day.

10. *Colicky babies are trying to manipulate their parents:* It's easy to fall into the trap of thinking a colicky baby is trying to "grab attention," that's she's demanding. Although infants as young as eight weeks do have a rudimentary understanding of cause and effect, that

if they cry someone will attend to their needs, they don't have the cognitive skills to manipulate their poor, unsuspecting folks. They're merely communicating that they're wet or hungry or physically or emotionally distressed by crying.

11. *Too much fresh air during the day can precipitate a colic attack during the evening or wee hours of the morning:* Just as your mother may have warned you to stay out of drafts—"or you might catch cold"—some people will caution that an afternoon outing to the park (and exposing baby to cool air) will trigger colicky symptoms later. Known as "wind colic," this myth has persisted throughout the years, but most parents find that rather than causing colic attacks, fresh air actually soothes their baby. Of course, this doesn't mean you should expose your baby to frigid air or leave his nursery window wide open on a brisk day, but fresh air definitely has no correlation with gassiness and irritability.

12. *Letting baby cry her lungs out is good for her; it will help increase her lung power:* While crying does have a psychological and physiological purpose (a good cry can relieve stress as well as increase a baby's body temperature when she's cold), prolonged crying has no real benefit. A screaming infant's heart rate can accelerate dramatically, and her throat will become irritated from constant wailing. Parents who are physically and emotionally exhausted may allow their baby to cry for fifteen to twenty minutes if everything else

has failed to calm the baby, and experts feel this is okay. But babies shouldn't be allowed to cry alone in their cribs for hours on end. Those who aren't regularly comforted when they cry may learn to distrust their caretakers—and the world around them.

13. *If your baby cries every evening, he definitely has colic:* Actually many babies—including noncolicky ones—have regular evening "cry times." Babies tend to cry at the end of the day to release the tension that's built up during the morning and early afternoon. The basic difference between the colicky and noncolicky infant is that the colicky one cries for three or more hours and is inconsolable.

14. *Breast-fed babies tend to have colic less often than formula-fed infants:* Studies show that equal numbers of breast-fed and formula-fed babies are colicky. The old belief that breast-feeding prevents colic can probably be traced to the theory that colic is an "intestinal problem" and that breast milk is easier to digest than formula. But since it is now felt that colic is linked to nervous-system problems (and not to gastrointestinal difficulties), this hypothesis can be laid to rest.

15. *Colicky infants spit up more often than noncolicky babies, and they are also more prone to diarrhea and/or constipation:* Research shows that colicky infants are no more likely than noncolicky babies to "spit up" or experience bouts of diarrhea and/or constipation. Occasionally a colicky baby may tend to spit up her food,

but this usually happens when the infant nurses every fifteen to thirty minutes and is literally filled up and overflowing.

16. *Thickening formula with a little cereal will help a colicky baby sleep through the night:* This myth derives from the notion that "solid foods" tend to induce sleep. Neither belief is true.

17. *Well-educated women are more likely to give birth to colicky babies:* One major study indicated that women with college (or nursing) degrees were more apt to have a colicky baby than women with a high-school education only. However, recent research refutes this theory and suggests that well-educated women are merely less hesitant about reporting their colicky baby's symptoms to pediatricians. Colic seems to have no connection with either a parent's education level or economic status.

6. Will Anything Stop the Crying?

It's ten minutes till midnight, and your baby has screamed relentlessly for two hours straight. You've tried every conceivable method of calming her, from bouncing her on your knee to swinging her high and low, to turning off all the nursery lights and holding her close, rocking her back and forth. As another wail pierces the otherwise still of the night, you're at the point of despair: "Will *anything* stop the crying?" you ask.

There are dozens of remedies—but, alas, no cures —for colic attacks. As discussed in chapter 4, your doctor may recommend a change in formula if you are bottle-feeding or, if you are nursing, suggest that you alter your own diet. In very severe cases of colic, some pediatricians prescribe medication for the agitated infant (we'll talk about "colic drugs" at the end of this chapter). But the remedies parents find most effective, and feel comfortable with, fall into the "it worked for me" category. These are simple colic management techniques parents swear by, from bundling up the cranky infant and taking him for a 2:00 A.M car ride to placing him tummy-down on a soothingly warm hot-water bottle.

Finding the method—or methods—that work best for your baby can be a guessing game. Keep in mind that every baby is different, and what works for one infant may not work for another. And, too, as one father remarked, "A particular method may not work all the time. What was effective on Monday didn't nec-essarily help the baby on Tuesday. Essentially, manag-ing her colic was a crapshoot!" Most parents find they need a whole repertoire of tricks when coping with in-fant colic, but they add this caveat: don't try too many techniques at the same time, or you'll merely end up overstimulating your baby! And, too, avoid jumping from one method to another—for instance, massaging baby's tummy for a few minutes and, when that doesn't work, desperately trundling her off to the me-chanical infant swing, and when that doesn't seem to help, bundling her up tightly in a blanket and franti-cally rocking her back and forth. It's best to give each method a fair trial to really determine if, in the long run, it works to calm your baby. Try to stick to a par-ticular technique for one or two days; if there's no change in your baby's behavior, test another remedy.

Whenever you find a method that seems to calm your infant even for as little as five minutes, write it down. Over the next few weeks you may find a pattern emerging: rocking little Andy seems effective in the evening, while he responds well to a tummy massage at 2:00 A.M.

You'll also need to determine what type of colicky infant your baby is. As mentioned before, there seem to be two kinds of colicky babies. The first responds to lots of stimulation and revels in being the center of attention. This baby may love daily massages or a morning dose of dancing in Mom's arms as rock and roll plays loudly in the background. The other baby, however, can't tolerate stimulation of any kind (except, perhaps, a car ride or other quiet, gentle, rhythmic motion) and will demand that you keep her environment utterly peaceful. She may be so sensitive to touch that even the gentlest massage will drive her wild, and if she likes music, she'll be happiest if you croon a barely audible lullaby.

As you observe your baby, you'll begin to tune in to her needs, and choosing the most appropriate colic-calmers will become easier.

Calming a Turbulent Tummy—No one knows for certain why any of the various colic methods works, but we can make some educated guesses. As mentioned earlier, gassiness (and cramping) seems to be a consequence—not a cause—of colic, and some parents find that techniques that provide gastric relief can help.

Change baby's feeding position: If you are breast-feeding, try holding your baby in a semisitting rather than a reclining position. If you are bottle-feeding, sit your baby upright in your lap or in an infant seat. An upright or semi-upright feeding position may allow food to pass more easily through baby's system and help him expel any pent-up gas.

Hold the bottle correctly: If you're bottle-feeding, or supplementing nursing with an occasional bottle, be sure to tilt the bottle upward so the nipple is always filled with liquid. If it isn't, baby will swallow air, increasing the chance of gassiness. For the same reason never let baby suck on an empty bottle.

Avoid overfeeding: Many colicky babies seem to want to nurse all the time. "My daughter wanted to nurse every fifteen to twenty minutes," recalls one mother. "It was a nightmare." Actually, overfeeding a colicky baby can do more harm than good; the infant who's "filled to the brim" is likely to spit up the excess or feel decidedly more uncomfortable after overeating. If your baby eats well at each feeding, try spacing her feedings every two-and-a-half to three hours. Between times, when she shows all the signs of a colic attack mounting, give her a pacifier or a little warm water in a bottle. It's probable that she just wants to suck, not eat.

Burp well—and often! Most parents burp their babies midway through a feeding and right after, but some infants, especially those who have spent a great deal of time crying and gulping air, need to be burped more frequently. Start by burping your baby *before* a feeding, then burp him several times during the feeding. Let him nurse a few minutes, and when he stops for a breather, burp him. Continue so throughout the feeding. There are two burping methods that work for most babies: Hold the baby over your shoulder and gently pat or rub his back until he brings up the air. Or sit him upright in your lap with his head resting against your chest and pat or rub his back.

If your baby seems to want to burp, but can't, lay him tummy-down for a minute or two, then try burping him again, using one of the above methods.

Check the nipple hole: If you're bottle-feeding, be sure the nipple hole isn't too large or too small, both of which can cause air gulping. The nipple should deliver a steady drip of liquid.

Let baby sleep tummy-down: Unless your baby is one of those who absolutely refuses to fall asleep on his tummy, place him belly-down in his crib. Experts feel babies tend to sleep longer and better in this position and that they spit up less and digest their food more easily.

Apply gentle pressure to baby's abdomen: To release pent-up gas, place baby tummy-down on a pillow or cushion, allowing her arms and legs to dangle slightly. Gently massage her back. Don't leave baby unattended, even if she falls asleep; she could easily roll off the pillow—and the sofa or bed!

Warm baby's tummy: Warmth, combined with gentle pressure on the abdomen, can break up gas bubbles. Place baby tummy-down on a comfortably warm hot-water bottle wrapped in a towel. Or, warm an over-sized bath towel in the clothes dryer, fold into squares, and place baby belly-down on the towel. Gently rub baby's back.

Try a soothing bath: While some colicky infants despise bath time, others find bathing relaxing. Gently immerse baby up to her shoulders in comfortably warm water and make lapping motions in the water with your free hand so that "warm waves" flow across her tummy (be sure you have a good hold on baby, with your free hand and arm supporting her shoulders, so she feels secure and doesn't slip into the water).

One parent reports that her baby loves to bathe *with* her. Carefully propped up in the tub, this mother holds her son next to her abdomen and chest and he seems to be soothed not only by the warm water, but the skin-to-skin contact with his mom as well.

Massage baby's tummy: According to one dad, tummy massages were among the few remedies that calmed his daughter. "Night after night, I put her back-down on a pillow," he says, "and rubbed her stomach while she hung on to the fingers of my free hand."

To massage your baby's tummy, place your palm over her navel (your fingers pointing downward toward her legs) and gently press with the heel of your hand as if you were "pushing" the gas out the rectum.

Before massaging baby's tummy, you might want to smooth a little baby oil onto her skin for extra comfort.

You can also use this massage technique while your baby is in a warm bath. As you massage her stomach, watch the bath water to see if bubbles appear; that's your clue that she is, indeed, passing gas!

Fennel tea soother: Folk remedies, especially "tea cures," have been used to calm colicky babies for hundreds of years. But parents should beware: many herbal teas are potentially toxic to babies (even some adults have experienced severe allergic reactions to certain herbal preparations, especially chamomile tea).

One herbal remedy, fennel tea, has been found to ease gastric distress in certain colicky babies, and though it's been used for years, the most recent report of its effectiveness comes from Varro Tyler, Ph.D., former dean of the School of Pharmacy at Purdue University. According to Tyler, the oil in fennel seeds dilates the blood vessels in the alimentary canal (the food tract, beginning with the esophagus and extending to the rectum and anus), expelling gas and producing a warming effect in the baby's digestive system.

To make fennel tea, pour four cups hot water over one teaspoon fennel seeds. Let steep for ten minutes, then strain out seeds. When the liquid has cooled, pour into a sterilized bottle and feed to baby.

Although weak fennel tea is presumed to be harmless, before you give this—or any other "natural" substance—to your baby, *check with your pediatrician.*

Soothing Motions, Sounds, and Gentle Restraint— Both rhythm (sound, motion) and restraint (swaddling, holding baby close) have a remarkably calming effect on colicky infants, and researchers speculate that these methods work because of some sort of interaction with the baby's central nervous system. As discussed in chapter 4, experts now feel that colicky babies are born with especially immature central nervous systems, and as a result, their brains send "faulty messages" to the various parts of their bodies. That's why these infants seem to lose control of their emotions—as well as their arms and legs and, possibly, equilibrium—and go into cataclysms of crying and thrashing around. They may also experience violent contractions of the gastrointestinal tract since the brain is sending inappropriate messages to that system, too.

The trick seems to be to interrupt or intercept those messages with external stimulation or restraint. Experts feel that motion, music, sucking, and lively or monotonous sounds all may help the baby regain some kind of control over his body, perhaps by momentarily distracting him from his discomfort and thus cutting short the messages his brain is sending to his body. Restraint also enables the baby to gain control over his wildly flailing arms and legs, and he's then better able to organize his world.

It's best to experiment with the different methods we've listed here. As mentioned earlier, one method may work for a day or two, then seem of no help, and you'll need to move on to another remedy to calm your baby.

Carrying: Numerous studies indicate that babies who are carried a great deal tend to cry less. Even three extra hours of carrying your baby each day may cut his cry time by 45 percent, and experts note that in some non-Western cultures, where babies are carried all day long, colic is virtually nonexistent. They hypothesize that the close proximity of the baby to his mother allows the parent to anticipate her child's needs, that the tiniest signs of hunger—squirming or rooting—alert Mom and allow her to feed her baby *before* he becomes uncomfortable and inconsolable.

But more important, a baby who is constantly close to his mother has the added benefit of hearing her heartbeat, feeling its gentle *lub-dub, lub-dub* against his chest, the same heartbeat he was so conscious of in the womb. The sound of a mother's heartbeat is rhythmic and soothing. It can also continuously interrupt or regulate the messages baby's brain is sending to his body.

The motion of carrying also serves a purpose in calming a baby. Your movements—walking, bending or stooping, climbing stairs—all provide external stimulation for the infant. Carrying is so effective in calming the colicky baby that some experts have gone so far as to suggest it's even more soothing than the old standby, feeding.

Try carrying your baby at least three hours a day, preferably *before* she begins to cry (if your baby has a routine cry time, you may be able to nip her crying spells in the bud by picking her up thirty minutes before one is due to begin).

Skin-to-skin contact: While bathing, or merely sitting in a rocking chair or lying on your bed, try holding your baby (unclothed) close to your chest or stomach. This method of soothing a colicky baby works well for both moms and dads, and some babies seem to prefer the interesting, hairy "texture" of their fathers' chests!

Recent research shows that skin-to-skin contact has an incredibly soothing effect on babies. And experts now feel that human touch actually induces a reduction of stress hormones in infants, children, and adults (touch also tells us we're safe; an infant who feels her parent's arms around her, or Mom's or Dad's chest pressed close to her own, will feel more secure and comforted).

Many parents report that wailing babies have fallen into a deep, serene sleep while lying tummy-down on a parent's chest. This is an ideal time, too, for you to catch up on your rest while you enjoy the closeness of your baby.

If your infant is prone to late-afternoon or early-evening colic attacks, you can try to offset them by nursing her half an hour before she usually launches into a tirade, then letting her snuggle up to your bare chest until she falls asleep. Gently place her in her crib and close the nursery door so she won't be disturbed by the sounds family members make as they return from school and work. Of course, you can keep tabs on baby with a nursery intercom.

Massage: Because touch is so effective in soothing a crying infant, many parents rely on a daily massage to help calm their colicky baby. Experts tend to agree that massage is beneficial, and you'll find numerous books about infant massage on the market, as well as a proliferation of "infant massage groups" or classes that meet regularly to explore the basic principles of baby massage.

While many babies do respond well to a gentle massage, remember that the ultrasensitive infant, the one who can't stand the slightest touch, probably won't appreciate this colic remedy.

It's best to begin massaging baby *before* she starts to cry, though a few infants can be calmed once they're past the whimpering stage. Try massaging your baby after she's nursed or been bathed and is feeling warm and soothed. Many parents like to gently rub a small amount of baby oil onto the infant's skin so their fingers glide over baby.

Lay baby either tummy- or back-down on a firm surface, such as a sofa, your bed, or a changing table, and use gentle, firm, slow strokes. If you touch baby too lightly, you run the risk of overstimulating—and even irritating—her. Each baby responds differently to a massage. Some prefer their tummies rubbed, while others adore a gentle stroking of their shoulders and lower back. You'll need to experiment a few times before you discover which areas to concentrate on, which ones to avoid. Gently stroke baby's arms and legs, then see if he minds having his feet and hands rubbed (because of the nerve endings in toes and fingers, some babies become annoyed when their feet or hands are touched).

You can massage your baby anywhere from five to

fifteen minutes, but she'll usually tell you when she's had enough. If she starts to squirm, that's your signal to stop.

For more information on infant massage, check your library or bookstore for these books: *Loving Hands* by Dr. Frederick Leboyer, *Infant Massage, a Loving Touch for Parents* by Vimala Schneider, *Baby Massage Book* by Tina Heinl, and *Baby Massage: Parent-Child Bonding Through Touch* by Amelia D. Auckett.

Pacifiers and warm water: Babies just naturally love to suck, and experts feel that the rhythmic motion of sucking can calm overwrought infants. Many of the mothers we talked to reported that their babies seemed "to want to nurse all the time." But when they fed their infants, the babies would suck for a few seconds or minutes, then spit out most of the liquid as if they were "filled to the brim." Often, a baby who's giving signals that he wants to eat—nuzzling at Mom's or Dad's chest, whimpering, searching for his fist or thumb—merely wants to suck, not eat. Sucking is one of the most soothing actions a baby can do himself (keep in mind that sucking and crying are totally incompatible; you can't do both at the same time!). Some experts have pointed out, too, that sucking not only helps a baby to block out internal and external stimuli, but pain as well.

Parents are sometimes reluctant to give their baby a pacifier, perhaps because they're afraid their child will still be sucking on one at the age of three! We should keep in mind, though, that if a baby—or toddler— truly wants to suck, he'll put anything into his mouth, be it a pacifier, his thumb, or the corner of a favorite blanket. And when a child no longer feels the need to suck on something, he's likely to give it up willingly.

The fact is, some colicky babies are calmed by pacifiers, and if you're able to quell your baby's wails by slipping a pacifier into his mouth—and sidestep a two-hour crying jag—you've done baby a kindness (and saved *yourself* from the agony of an all-out colic attack).

It's best to give your baby a pacifier before he starts to cry and thrash. Look for general signs of restlessness, then gently ease the pacifier into his mouth before he has time to start wailing. One important caution: Never hang a pacifier, attached to a ribbon or cord, around baby's neck. Either the pacifier or cord could get caught in the rung's of baby's crib or play yard, and strangulation could occur. Also, ask your pediatrician to recommend a good brand of pacifier, one that's shaped to ensure proper development of your baby's jaws and teeth, and meets U.S. Consumer Product Safety Commission standards. (Safe pacifiers have a wide mouthguard with a securely attached nipple to prevent choking. The mouthguard should have at least two ventilation holes and a large handle.)

Some parents find that giving baby a little warm water in a bottle helps to soothe him. In fact, a baby will often continue to suck even after he's fallen asleep and the bottle has been removed from his mouth. This sleep sucking seems to be baby's way of unconsciously calming himself.

Swaddling: The practice of swaddling newborns is centuries old and most of us are familiar with the phrase "Wrap the babe in his swaddling clothes," long, narrow bands of cloth snugly secured around the infant.

Swaddling is a form of restraint that helps the baby who has lost his sense of equilibrium regain a feeling of being in control. The wildly agitated infant who can't stop swinging his arms and legs or seems desperately trying to regain his balance can often be calmed by swaddling. Also, the ultrasensitive infant who doesn't like too much stimulation, who would rather shut out the world and literally be wrapped up in a cocoon, can benefit from swaddling.

Many parents report that their colicky infants quiet down when they're carried in one of the cloth front packs that are so popular. Of course, a front pack allows the baby to rest against Mom's or Dad's chest, to hear the soothing sounds of a parent's heartbeat and breathing. But often, an infant will pull his legs and arms into the pack, all "tucked in." Perhaps he feels as though he's back in the warm, secure comfort of the womb, the ultimate in swaddling.

Other parents find their babies like to cuddle up in infant sleeping bags, another form of swaddling clothes. If you do try a sleeping bag, keep an eye on baby so she doesn't get too warm or suddenly wake up feeling trapped.

Still other parents say a modified version of the traditional swaddling procedure works best. To swaddle your baby, place her in the center of a light, soft blanket with her head and feet pointing toward opposite corners. Fold the bottom corner up over her feet and pull in the sides so they're wrapped around her arms (she may pull her arms up to her chest so they gently nestle there). If your baby truly needs to shut out the world, use the top corner of the blanket as a hood. You can carry or rock your baby once she's swaddled, or lie on the sofa or bed, holding her close.

Be sure, though, that the swaddling blanket isn't too tight and baby doesn't become too warm.

Infant swing: Mechanical infant swings, the ones you wind up and let run for ten or fifteen minutes, are lifesavers for many parents of colicky infants. Says one dad, "The only way my wife and I could eat dinner in relative peace was to put our daughter in her swing. We kept it by the dining-room table, and she'd swing back and forth, eyeing us—but with no smile—just being very quiet. As soon as the swing stopped, if she hadn't fallen asleep and we could see her begin to squirm, one of us would jump up from the table, crank up the swing—and all would be well for another ten minutes!"

One caution about infant swings: Never leave your baby unattended even for a minute. Also, make sure he's securely strapped in, with both waist and crotch belts.

If you can find a swing that plays a tune, so much

the better. The combination of swinging and music seems particularly calming to some babies.

The colic "throw": Sudden, but smooth and rhythmic changes in elevation sometimes distract babies from their troubles. One mother reports that her husband "would strap Susan in her infant seat and swing her high and low, back and forth. Sometimes I was afraid she'd shoot off like a missile if Mark ever accidentally let go! I think the swinging sort of startled her out of her crying fit."

Walking up and down stairs with your baby may also help. Parents do say they're often so exhausted that climbing stairs is just too tiring. But if you can manage it, you'll not only calm your baby, but work in a little aerobic exercise for yourself as well!

The airplane hold: Many dads like to rock or swing their babies in the "airplane hold" or "airplane position." Hold baby tummy-down, supporting her chest with one hand and her legs with the other. Rock or swing her back and forth, either gently or vigorously, depending on the tempo she prefers.

The colic cradle: Another favorite of dads is the colic hold or cradle. Stretch baby out horizontally tummy-down along your arm, with her head at your elbow and your hand cupped between her dangling legs. Use your other hand to hold the top of her buttocks or thighs. You can walk baby in this position, or swing her.

The colic dance: Babies who like stimulation respond well to the age-old colic dance, where a parent holds the child close to her chest and moves back and forth, side to side, and up and down. Some infants enjoy a parent's gentle humming during the dance. Others prefer soothing classical music, and a few tune in to rock and roll. Experiment with different musical selections to see which ones work best for your baby; also, try different tempos while you dance. While a slow, smooth, gliding gait works best for one child, another baby may calm down more quickly if your movements are fairly rapid and somewhat jerky.

Car rides: One of the most effective ways of calming a baby who's totally out of control is to strap her in her car seat and take her for a ride. Says one mother, "Even though we live in New York City and it's a hassle to get our car out of the apartment-building garage, there *have* been times when we've packed all three kids into the car—just to calm the colicky one!"

Both the smooth, but vibrating motion of an automobile as well as the sound of the engine (and, perhaps, traffic noises) can instantly calm even the crankiest infants. And the blur of fleeting sights seems to distract them from their woes as well. Many a parent who's close to desperation has bundled up his colicky baby and taken her for a 2:00 A.M. drive!

The "colic machine": One dad who'd been pushed beyond his limits by his son's incessant crying went so far as to make an emergency 2:30 A.M. trip to the baby's pediatrician, only to notice that the motion and sound of the car lulled the screaming infant to sleep. As a result, the father, Armando Cuervo, developed a device called SleepTight℠, a vibration unit that attaches to the springs of a crib and a noise unit that emulates the sound of wind whooshing past the closed windows of a car.

SleepTight℠, which was funded by the National Institute of Child Health and Human Development's Special Business Innovation Research Grants program, has been approved as a medical device by the Food and Drug Administration, and the machine's effectiveness rate in calming colicky babies is impressive. After a three-year trial by pediatricians and psychologists, SleepTight℠ was found to lessen symptoms in fifty-eight of sixty infants; 85 percent of the babies stopped crying four minutes after the machine was turned on. A second study of forty colicky infants showed that the device also greatly relieved maternal anxiety and distress.

For more information about the "colic machine," speak with your pediatrician.

A stroll around the block: Colicky babies tend to be happiest outdoors, and although we don't know for certain why fresh air seems to quiet them, we can guess that they're distracted by the scents in the air as well as slight breezes and the hustle-bustle of everyday life.

And, too, the rhythm of a stroller or carriage as it rolls along the sidewalk serves as a distraction. One mother remembers taking her daughter for stroller rides every day (even at 11:00 P.M.!), but adds that the baby was born during the summer, so a few laps around the block on a warm day or night were feasible.

In bad weather, when you're confined to the house, put your baby in a carriage or stroller and wheel him through the various rooms. The motion may calm him to the point that he drifts off to sleep, and if he does, don't disturb him by carrying him to his crib. Let him sleep in the stroller or carriage.

Jiggling and bouncing: Babies who appreciate stimulation like being jiggled or bounced on a parent's knee (be sure you're gentle, though, or you could agitate baby even more). If you have a baby carriage with "springs," jiggle the handle to create a slight vibrating motion (you can sit while you do this and use your free hand to hold a paperback novel; remember, you deserve a little escape time, too).

Knee scissors: Place baby tummy-down across your knees and move them up and down in a scissorlike motion. Keep a good hold on baby's back with one hand (this method is particularly helpful when you're trying to eat, but must hold baby at the same time).

Put baby on the clothes dryer: One of the most ingenious methods of soothing a baby who's already in the throes of a good squall is to buckle her into an infant seat or car seat and set it on top of a running clothes dryer. Of course, you must hold the seat so it doesn't creep to the edge of the dryer—and you can never leave baby unattended, even for a second.

Another calming technique is to spread a folded blanket on top of the dryer and place baby on it tummy down. She'll feel the warmth from the dryer on her belly and get a "whole body massage" at the same time. Again, be sure you have a good grip on baby and never leave her unattended.

Play music or monotonous-sound records or tapes: Many parents find that certain types of music soothe their wailing infants, in particular, pieces with a definite regular bass-line rhythm of about sixty beats per minute (baroque instrumental music is especially effective). Music seems to "hypnotize" or calm both infants and adults by regulating their heartbeats and allowing them to enter deeply relaxed states or fall asleep. Some parents also recommend "nature" records or tapes, sounds of waves crashing against rocks and sea gulls crying in the background, or birds singing in a forest.

Others say that womb sounds can sometimes quiet a colicky infant, recordings of heartbeats and whooshing noises, similar to the sounds a baby hears while in the womb. Recalls one mom, "Someone gave us a recording of a mother's heartbeat and the sound of blood rushing through the placenta. On the other side of the record were beautiful lullabies. I listened to the first side, the *lub-dub*, *lub-dub* and *whoosh-whoosh*, *whoosh-whoosh*, and said, 'I'll be darned if I give in and play this silly thing for my child!'

"Then, one morning at about 2:00 A.M., when my husband and I had been up for what seemed like hours with our baby, we both started to laugh and said almost simultaneously, 'Well, it's time for the record!' And it worked, at least for a little while."

White noise: While music and heartbeat records work for some babies, others—especially those who are super-sensitive—unwind to *extremely* monotonous, nonmusical, almost nonrhythmic noise. Some parents have found that their babies suddenly calm down when they hear the sound of a vacuum cleaner. Of course, you won't want to run your vacuum cleaner every day for thirty minutes or longer, but you *can* record the sound and play it for baby just before he's due to launch into a colic attack.

Other babies tune out when they hear the static on a television or radio station that's gone off the air, and some like the noise made by a whirring fan or air conditioner. Still others prefer the sound of running water, from either the faucet or shower. Says one mother, "I put my daughter in her stroller (set for sleep position) and wheeled her into the hallway just outside the bathroom, then turned on the shower full blast. The sound of rushing water was one of the few things that soothed her (I finally taped the running shower so I could play it to her when she'd wake up at 3:00 A.M.), and to this day, she's fascinated by the sight and sound of waterfalls on Public Television's 'Nature' series!"

Controlling baby's environment: As mentioned earlier, some babies can't tolerate any stimulation. Sights, sounds, and movements—like the colic dance or swinging—can all make these babies even more irritated and anxious than they were to begin with. If your baby is one of these little hermits, do keep in mind that he'll "emerge" once the colic subsides. But for the time being, give him the space—and peace and quiet —he needs in order to gain some feeling of control.

Keep lights in the nursery (as well as other parts of the house) on the dimmest setting. For babies who demand complete darkness, invest in blackout blinds or drapes for the nursery. Family members will need to talk in hushed tones around this type of infant, and many parents will find that they spend hours on end in a darkened, quiet room, gently rocking or merely holding their baby until she falls asleep.

Although your family and friends will want to see your new baby, if he's ultrasensitive, don't subject him to a deluge of visitors. On the other hand, if a relative or friend offers to relieve you for an hour or longer, let her comfort your baby while you get some well-deserved rest!

When All Else Fails—It's likely that there will be times when nothing you do will calm your baby, and after hours of trying to comfort her, it's perfectly all right to put her in her crib and let her cry for fifteen minutes while you recoup your strength (and your sanity!). By this time, the baby may be so overwrought, she might not notice you're taking a breather.

Although one mother tells of letting her son "cry it out—and then feeling terribly guilty when he sobbed himself to sleep in his crib," there's little need to feel guilt about taking a break from baby once in a while. After all, you're with him 95 percent of the time (more than most parents of noncolicky babies!) and a fifteen-minute break now and then is essential for your physical and emotional well-being.

Colic Drugs—No discussion of colic remedies would be complete without mention of the various medications doctors have prescribed over the years to relieve colic symptoms. And while drug therapy has lost favor with the medical profession, some doctors do resort to medications, usually when the colic is so severe neither baby nor parent is getting any rest.

When a child appears to have severe gastrointestinal difficulties, pediatricians sometimes prescribe simethicone drops, a liquid formulation of the same medication adults take in pill form to break up gas bubbles. Certain babies do experience relief after taking the drops, though others fail to show any letup in symptoms.

Over the years, physicians have attempted to relax both the central nervous system and the gastrointestinal tract of colicky babies with various sedatives, especially phenobarbital. This drug was most popular during the 1950's but a few doctors still prescribe it today. However, phenobarbital can have dangerous side effects, including a slowing of breathing and pulse rate, and it may adversely affect the central nervous system. Also, babies who are given the drug spend much of their "alert" time drugged up in a sleepy, lethargic state.

The only medication approved as effective in the

treatment of colic by the Food and Drug Administration is dicyclomine hydrochloride, a muscle relaxant that relieves cramping in the gastrointestinal tract but may have a relaxing effect on the central nervous system as well. Generally prescribed for the most serious cases of colic, the drug is not a narcotic, barbiturate, tranquilizer, or sedative and the side effects are fewer than those of drugs such as phenobarbital (reactions to dicyclomine include sluggishness, decreased appetite, constipation, rashes, and urine retention). Dicyclomine can be extremely effective—when it works. And that's the catch: The medication relieves symptoms of colic in some babies, not at all in others.

Finally, in past decades, some doctors advised parents to give their unhappy infants "a little whiskey in sugar water" to literally knock out the baby. This colic "cure" has carried over to the present day, but it's usually a well-meaning but misinformed relative or friend who offers the advice now. Babies should never, under any circumstances, be given alcohol; the substance can seriously lower the infant's blood sugar level, adversely affect the central nervous system, and possibly cause coma.

7. Taking Care of Yourself

We've called this chapter "Taking Care of Yourself" because moms and dads need just as much understanding, attention, love, and care as baby. And, too, even though you may not be a first-time parent, if you're the mother or father of a colicky infant, in a sense you are a "new" parent. Caring for the colicky baby is infinitely more difficult than taking care of the noncolicky baby, and you'll need to redefine your own definition of what it means to be a *good parent*. Says one mother, "When my daughter was born, I was supermom. But with my colicky son, I threw everything out the window I'd learned regarding parenting! I found myself sitting on the couch next to my husband and crying, saying, 'I'm not a good mother anymore.' And I hated to ask anyone to help me take care of Mark. I had a very hard time admitting I couldn't manage him—when I'd done so well with my first child."

The "good enough parent": Becoming a parent is one of the most stressful life events anyone faces. Becoming the parent of a colicky baby can magnify that stress tenfold. The first step parents of a colicky infant must take is to get rid of any unrealistic expectations of being "supermom" or "superdad," and accept the fact that under these least of ideal circumstances, you're going to be a "good enough parent." That means you'll do your best in caring for your infant, even though life has handed you a raw deal. And being the parents of a colicky baby is a raw deal, it's unfair, and you're perfectly justified in feeling angry and frustrated because your illusions about having a "perfect little baby" have collided head on with reality.

What's more, as parents of a colicky infant, you're likely to feel tired most of the time. The first weeks and months of taking care of a baby are exhausting and confusing, and when the baby is colicky, parents are often so exhausted they move around in a trance-like state. After a 2:00 A.M. to 4:00 A.M. stint of comforting your baby, just getting up in the morning, taking off your nightgown or pajamas, and putting on "grown-up" clothes can be a daunting task. Things that once seemed easy are now major undertakings.

Mothers especially have a difficult time. After giving birth, a woman's body will need time to heal and she'll find her energy is much lower than usual. Though most new mothers begin to feel more like their prepregnancy selves by the sixth or seventh week after delivery, those who've had cesareans or complicated deliveries may take longer to regain their stamina. And, too, during the first few weeks, hormones are shifting dramatically and a mother may feel "down" or unusually sensitive or irritable. Some women find they cry more easily, or alternately feel joy and sadness about becoming mothers. Doctors call this reaction postpartum depression or the "baby blues," and though for most women these few days or weeks of mood swings aren't anything to worry about, some new mothers do suffer from serious depressions. Having a colicky baby can exacerbate even mild feelings of depression and helplessness, and the effects of fatigue (caused by staying up all night with the baby) can even mimic a more serious case of the baby blues. We'll talk more about ways to minimize fatigue and stress, but in the meantime, it's wise for new moms to determine whether feelings of hopelessness and helplessness are caused mostly by fatigue and the demands of managing a colicky infant or by postpartum depression, which can be treated by a doctor.

If you continue to have any of these symptoms after the first few weeks following delivery, talk to your obstetrician to rule out postpartum depression:

• Extreme feelings of anger, hostility toward your child, partner, and other people (especially those who comment about your parenting ability).

• A feeling of being on edge all the time, of being "wired," or jumpy or nervous, as though your mind and body are "racing."

• Lack of pleasure in activities you previously enjoyed.

• Disinterest in seeing people you usually like being around.

• Loss of appetite.

• Feeling guilty and worthless as a parent—and a human being.

• Experiencing no joy or contentment, and feeling as though life isn't worth living.

Putting your own needs on hold: New parents tend to focus almost solely on their baby, often pushing their own needs—for love, attention, relaxation, and fun—to the background. As the parent of a colicky infant, it's not uncommon to inadvertently allow your life to revolve almost totally around your baby at the expense of your relationship with your spouse, friends, and family. A colicky baby can truly become an obsession; you worry constantly about her health (as one mother says, "The first week after my daughter was born, I was in a panic. She cried for what seemed like twenty-four hours a day and I was certain she must be *seriously* ill. My mother had to reassure me over and over that the baby simply had colic—and that she was perfectly normal."); you become so concerned that the baby get enough to eat, you forget to eat yourself (or grab a piece of cheese and a cracker for dinner because you couldn't put the baby down long enough to prepare, much less eat, a meal); and whereas you may have enjoyed reading (novels, the newspaper, magazines), you find you can't concentrate for more than one or two minutes on any reading material since you've become so used to being interrupted by baby's demanding wail. In essence, you forget that you're a human being, too, who needs a lot of TLC during this extremely stressful period, and you automatically put your life "on hold" for three or four months.

Feeling a sense of isolation: Mothers of colicky babies experience a profound sense of isolation. Most fathers receive only a few days (or, in the most ideal circumstances, two weeks) of paternity leave from their companies, and even those who do get time off are hesitant to take advantage of it for fear of displeasing management. (It's sad but true, many employers resent granting maternity leave to working women, and make it clear to dads-to-be that though the company may have a paternity-leave policy, they'd prefer the man didn't take the time off. We know of one boss who, looking thirty years back to the birth of his children, remarked, "*I* never got time off when my wife and I had our kids. Why should I let 'Mike' take off two weeks?") This kind of attitude leaves the new mother on her own to cope, unless *her* mother or another relative or baby nurse moves in to help care for the baby during the first few weeks. And after that, Mom is essentially alone; everyone abandons her—especially if the baby turns out to be colicky.

"I felt so alone," recalls the mother of a colicky boy. "I didn't know any other young mothers in my neighborhood. There was no one I could talk to about what I was going through." The mother of a colicky infant not only feels house-bound, she also lacks a good support system—other parents who can understand the problems she's facing. The camaraderie that naturally springs up between mothers of noncolicky babies, moms who meet regularly in the park or chat over a cup of coffee, doesn't exist for mothers of colicky babies. One of the most frustrating things the mother of a colicky infant faces is seeing other mothers with "normal," happy, chortling babies. Says one mom, "I resented them. I wished I had a baby who acted nice and happy. These other mothers didn't have a clue as to what I was experiencing." So, the mother of the colicky baby often feels alone, not only physically alone with her screaming baby, but emotionally alone as well, with no one to really confide in.

Accepting negative feelings: As parents, we don't "like" ourselves very much when we experience unacceptable feelings about our children, feelings of dislike, anger, or something approaching outright hatred. But even the best of parents occasionally can't stand their children, and the parents of colicky infants are likely to feel negatively about their babies quite a bit of the time, especially when those parents are exhausted.

In a recent essay in *The New York Times Magazine*, a physician tells how he repeatedly reassured parents of colicky infants that their babies were entirely normal and that in three or four months the colic would pass and everything would be fine. But after the birth of his colicky daughter, the doctor felt such raging hostility toward the screaming baby he confessed to a group of other physicians that he "hated" his child, that he wanted "to shake her till she shut up!"

A mother echoes this doctor's sentiments. Says Judy, "I'm usually an upbeat person, and I was just fine with my first son. But when my second little boy turned out to be colicky, I really couldn't stand him. He made me depressed about being a mother." Judy remembers hearing a grisly news report about a woman who had confessed to drowning her two-month-old baby. "My husband and I were listening to the radio and were horrified to hear that a parent could do such an awful thing," she says. "Then we heard the newscaster say, 'Authorities feel the child may have had a severe case of colic,' and we turned to each other and simultaneously said, 'Well, that could do it!'"

Of course, parents of colicky infants rarely go so far as to harm their babies, but often the feeling of wanting to "shut the child up" is there. It's best to accept the fact that you may have uncomfortable feelings of anger and hostility, even though you've never been prone to them before. (Says one mother, "I couldn't even bring myself to spank my dog, even when he tore up the kitchen, but suddenly here I was feeling uncontrollable rage when my baby screamed her head off. I found myself thinking nasty things, like 'I can't stand you, you little brat! I'd like to throw you down the stairs!'")

There are ways to defuse the anger you may feel toward your baby, but if you do get to the point where you're so overwhelmed and out of control that you think you might possibly harm your child, get help. Talk to a counselor, therapist, your obstetrician, or a clergy person. Or look in the front section of your phone book (community service numbers) for the number of the local child-abuse hotline.

Managing your relationship: Most couples find that after the birth of their first child they need to redefine their roles as husband and wife. And as parents of a colicky baby, you'll need to spend time nurturing your relationship, which will inevitably take a backseat to baby. All too often, parents are so preoccupied with the baby and her problems that they tend to forget about each other and their mutual needs. Also, because they're exhausted and irritable, they may find themselves arguing with each other over unimportant things, such as who should do what around the house, or criticizing each other's parenting styles. "We were constantly bickering," says one mother, who—like her husband—is a psychotherapist. "We were practically at each other's throats all the time. I felt as though Brian was shirking his responsibility with the baby; he set up appointments with patients that ran late into the evening and I was stuck at home all day with our screaming daughter.

"When Brian walked through the door at 9:00 or 10:00 P.M., I'd shove Tamara into his arms and say, 'You take her, or either she or I won't be around much longer!'"

This same mother also recalls that she and her husband became critical of each other's parenting styles. "Tamara seemed to want to nurse all the time, but her doctor said she was growing normally and didn't need to eat every twenty minutes. But Brian insisted Tamara wasn't getting enough milk, and that really tapped into my insecurities about being a first-time mother. He and I were pitted against each other over so many things like that. There was a lot of fighting, even though, as psychotherapists, we realized we should take time out and talk things over rationally. It's just that when you're operating on zero sleep, you forget to think rationally!"

One of the most common traps parents of colicky babies fall into is forgetting that they are partners, not adversaries. Talking, sharing your feelings and fears with one another, is crucial. And so is setting aside "togetherness time," thirty minutes a day, or an hour or two a week, that you spend by yourselves while someone else cares for baby.

Learning to be your own parent: It's unrealistic to expect that as parents we'll become the primary focus of friends and family, that these people will lavish us with TLC. Relatives and friends just naturally focus on the new baby, and when the baby is colicky, they offer advice about how to comfort *him*. But parents need comforting—and caring—too. And often, we have to make the decision to nurture ourselves. Although the advice, "take good care of yourself" may sound simple, most of us ignore it during times of extreme stress. Here, tips on being a good parent—to yourself!

1. Accept your ambivalent feelings about baby. Don't feel as though you must "love" your baby right away. It's difficult to summon up affection, almost on command, for a colicky infant who is often (and, in some cases, totally) unresponsive to you, a baby who rarely smiles or chortles, or who doesn't snuggle happily against your chest. As Maria says, "My son didn't like to cuddle; he was stiff as a board and cried all the time. I didn't like him very much and it was hard to feel the 'love' I felt early on for my first child."

Just as you can't expect to feel deep love for someone you meet for the first time, don't berate yourself if you don't experience a strong loving attachment to your baby during his colicky phase. Of course, some moms and dads do "fall in love" with baby at first sight, but for most of us, loving our children is a gradual, day-to-day process. As we get to know our baby over weeks and months, our attachment deepens, until one day we realize we couldn't live without him. And parents of colicky babies should realize that unless the baby's colic is very mild, that attachment process may take more time. As one mother recalls, "My son cried, literally, for twenty-four hours a day, and until the colic passed, we really didn't form a strong bond. But now we're very close. I love that little boy!"

2. Be realistic about your feelings. Admit to yourself that your baby isn't the ideal, that she isn't the placid, cooing infant you pictured as you awaited her birth. Then tell yourself it's okay to be disappointed and frustrated. If you try to submerge these feelings—and put on a happy face for your partner, friends, and rela-

tives—you may end up feeling even more resentful because you're living a lie.

3. When you're feeling particularly angry because you're "saddled" with a nonstop wailer (or you feel increasingly mad at baby), take a piece of paper and write down all the things about your child that you can't stand. Or simply write or type, "I can't take this kid anymore, I can't take this kid anymore," as many times as you need to release your pent-up anger. (One mother we talked to typed, "I hate her! I hate her!" one hundred times and felt immense relief afterward.) Then cut up your list into dozens of pieces or wad it up and throw it in the trash.

This is a good, concrete way of venting your anger, then literally "getting rid of it."

4. There may be days when you want to scream at your baby, "Shut up! Why are you doing this to me?" (or some other negative sentiment). Try cuddling your infant, and in the sweetest tone of voice you can summon, with a smile on your face, tell her everything that you can't stand about her behavior. She'll pick up on your tone and facial expression, but won't understand what you're saying, and you'll safely release your rage.

5. On a piece of paper, list all the positive things your baby has done today (for example, "Linda smiled at me this morning," or "Gerry didn't cry at 10:00 A.M. like she usually does," or "I love to look at Michael when he sleeps; his little fingers and toes curl up like

an elf's"). If you can't think of anything positive to write about your infant on a particular day, list the things you think she'll do when she's past her colicky stage (for instance, "Mary will smile so much more in a couple of months," or "She'll snuggle in my arms and nurse for a good twenty minutes, then drift off into a peaceful sleep").

Whenever you're feeling as though your baby will never outgrow her colic, take a few minutes to read through your list and make an effort to really believe what you've recorded.

6. Practice visualizing or "imaging" the way your baby will be when she's four or five months old and the colic has subsided. Sit in a quiet room and breathe slowly and deeply until you feel relaxed. Picture your baby as an older infant, smiling and cooing; then visualize her as a toddler, and, perhaps, as a preschooler. Make your visualizations as concrete as possible, noticing the adorable outfit she's wearing, what fun she's having playing in her sandbox, the way she interacts with you. Visualizing your baby in a positive manner will help you focus on the "light at the end of the tunnel," reminding you that colic does indeed end, and perhaps more important, you'll be laying the groundwork for a positive relationship with your child.

7. Whenever you begin to feel your baby is "demanding," that she's trying to manipulate you or is sending you messages that you're not a "good parent," repeat over and over to yourself, "My baby doesn't hate me. She's not trying to manipulate me. What seems like

her 'anger' isn't directed at me. She just doesn't feel well."

8. Share both your positive and negative feelings about your baby not only with your partner but with an understanding relative or friend. There's no need to hide your true feelings out of the fear that you'll be judged less of a parent for telling the truth. When a good friend asks, "Even though Johnny cries a lot, aren't you ecstatic about having him?" tell her that although you're happy to have a healthy baby, it's very difficult parenting an infant who cries all day long, and that there are times when you're so upset and tense you aren't able to focus on the "joys" of parenthood.

A truly good friend will sympathize with you, though she may not be able to put herself in your place unless she's had a colicky baby herself.

9. If you begin to feel desperately depressed or hopeless or unable to care for your baby, don't hesitate to seek help. Arlene, who's the mother of a formerly colicky baby and is also a psychotherapist, says, "Talking to a trained therapist or counselor, a third party who's not emotionally involved with your child like you and your partner, can help you put things into perspective and allow you to learn coping strategies you might not have thought of while you were so despondent—and felt so alone." To find a good counselor, call a mental health clinic or family health clinic in your area. Some women's centers also have family therapists on staff. You can also ask your doctor to recommend a private therapist.

10. Create your own support network. Join a parents' support group. It's likely two or three members will be parents of colicky children and you can arrange to meet informally with these moms and dads at your house or a restaurant to talk about what you're going through, share tips on coping with colic. (Your pediatrician may be a good source as well; she can connect you with other parents of colicky babies.)

If you aren't able to find parents who are currently experiencing the "colic crisis," talk to people whose children *were* colicky. They can give you tried-and-true tips on managing colic, and also assure you that colic does pass. Says one father, "My wife had a friend whose baby was colicky for six months; the kid screamed all day long. By talking with her, we knew we'd live through the experience, and since our daughter wasn't as colicky as hers, we realized what we were going through could be worse!"

11. Make relaxation a major priority. You're bound to feel physically drained much of the time. As one mother says, "Going without sleep is incredibly stressful. I was so tense for months that I often couldn't nurse when the baby demanded to eat—the milk just wouldn't come. And I was so tired I couldn't think clearly either. I'd walk around like a zombie and wonder if I'd fed the baby or if I'd forgotten!" Fatigue leads to irritability, disorientation (you may wonder where you put baby's wet diaper, only to find it days later, stuffed into her dresser drawer instead of the diaper pail!), sensitivity to others' comments about not

only your parenting style but your appearance as well (if your mother remarks that you "look tired," you're apt to snap, "Well, you'd look a wreck, too, if you'd been up all night!"), and a feeling of being out of control or helpless.

One of the best ways to relax, to relieve both physical and mental stress—and prepare yourself to care for your baby—is to meditate. You may want to read Dr. Herbert Benson's classic, *The Relaxation Response*, for an in-depth explanation of meditation principles, or you can follow this simple exercise. It's best to choose a time of day when you're 95 percent sure baby will be asleep, then unplug your phone so you won't be disturbed.

• Choose a quiet room and sit in a comfortable chair (your back should be straight, your feet flat on the floor, your hands resting comfortably at your sides or in your lap). If you want absolute privacy, take a straight-back chair into the bathroom, close the door, and run water in the sink or shower to blot out any noise!

• Begin to breathe in deeply, allowing the air to fill your diaphragm. As you slowly exhale, imagine all your cares and responsibilities passing out with your breath. You can say a word or sound with each exhalation if you like. Some people focus on the word *one* or the sound *om*, while others choose peace-evoking words like *serene* or *serenity*. (Instead of repeating a word, you might try focusing on an imaginary, calming scene such as a still lake, or a candle.)

• As worries (about baby, chores that must be done) pop into your mind, gently refocus your thoughts on the word you're repeating or scene you are visualizing.

• After a few minutes, begin to contract, then relax your muscles, starting with your neck and shoulders, progressing to your chest, your stomach, your arms and hands, your upper and lower legs, and finally your feet and toes. Then imagine a warm wave moving from the top of your head, down through your body (you can give the wave a color, if you like).

• When you're thoroughly relaxed, you might want to lie down for fifteen or twenty minutes more to catch a quick nap while baby sleeps.

If possible, meditate for fifteen or twenty minutes every day to relieve tension, recharge physically and emotionally.

12. Retreat to the bathroom for "time out." When your baby finally falls asleep (or your partner or a sitter is relieving you), indulge in a long shower or bath. If you're showering, set the shower attachment for "pulsating" and aim the jets of water at the tense, taut muscles in your upper back and shoulders. If you opt for a long, soothing bath, make sure you have a portable radio or cassette recorder in the bathroom so you can listen to calming music. Music will mask noises from outside, as well as anywhere in the house, and allow you to concentrate fully on yourself.

Interestingly, one researcher has found that people who take long showers show a significant reduction in anxiety and tension levels.

13. Exercise is another excellent way to alleviate stress and fatigue, defuse feelings of anger and helplessness. Studies show that aerobic exercise elevates mood, creates a sense of well-being by triggering the release of certain hormones in the body (one recent study indicated that even a slow, twelve-minute walk can reduce tension and anxiety).

New moms should take it easy, though; for the first six weeks after giving birth, the most you should do are very gentle stretches, shoulder and ankle circles, and moderate walking. (If you've had a cesarean or any postpregnancy complications, you'll need even more time for your body to heal and your stamina to return.) After six weeks, many women find they can ease back into prepregnancy exercise routines, including jogging and swimming. (Of course, it's wise to check with your doctor before beginning any exercise program.)

Ideally, both Mom and Dad should try to set aside twenty to thirty minutes a day for exercise.

14. "Tune out" when you're worn out! If, after an hour or more of carrying and consoling your screaming infant, you think you can't possibly take one more minute of the torture—but are reluctant to put baby in her crib—slip a tape into your cassette player, put on your earphones, and lose yourself in the music (rock and roll is loudest and will effectively drown out baby's cries, though classical organ pieces and Sousa marching tunes will muffle the noise as well). You'll still have

the close body contact with your child, but her cries will be barely audible.

15. If time and finances permit, treat yourself to a Swedish or Japanese pressure-point massage (shiatsu). Research has shown that human touch can induce a reduction in stress hormones, and a weekly massage will go a long way in helping you feel better both physically and mentally. You and your partner can also learn the basics of pressure-point massage (there are numerous how-to books available), and by simply rubbing and kneading each other's tense shoulders and back muscles, you can reduce stress while you spend valuable time together.

16. Take a break from critical people. Begin consciously to ignore critical remarks or well-meant but misguided advice from relatives or friends. For example, if your aunt tells you you're spoiling your baby by picking him up when he begins to cry, but you feel uncomfortable leaving him sobbing piteously in his crib, follow your instincts, comfort your baby, and either ignore your aunt's advice or tell her you prefer to hold your child. If she continues to criticize your parenting methods or expresses disapproval with comments such as, "Well, if I were you, I'd..." simply change the subject so she knows the matter is not open for discussion.

You need friends and relatives who give you support and encouragement, not criticism, and though it isn't possible to "banish" irritating people from your home (especially relatives and close friends), do feel free to cut short their visits with, "I'm feeling tired all of a sudden. Now that the baby's asleep, I think I'll go upstairs for a nap, too."

Also, try to surround yourself with helpful, supportive friends. Their sympathy and nonjudgmental attitude can offset the more critical comments of others.

17. Baby yourself. Both moms and dads should regularly reward themselves for being "good enough parents." The rewards can be simple things, like a Saturday afternoon spent golfing or a morning devoted to shopping for a new outfit. New mothers, especially, need to pamper themselves, and often that includes treating yourself to something that will improve your appearance and boost your morale (when you look good, you tend to feel good). One mom remembers being so exhausted and forgetful that there were times when she didn't get dressed until noon. "I literally lived in my nightgown, and if someone came to the door, I was horrified to find I hadn't had time to put on jeans and a sweatshirt." She adds, ruefully, that jeans and sweats were her "dress-up clothes."

Buying a new pair of slacks or shoes, having your hair cut in a different style, or taking an hour out of your hectic day for a manicure or pedicure will lift your flagging spirits.

18. Don't be afraid to vent your emotions. If you feel the need to have a good cry, do so (some more reserved parents hesitate to shed tears in public, even in

front of their partners, and for them the answer can be to lock themselves in the bathroom, run water full force in the sink, and indulge in a stress-relieving sob). Just as baby's tears help release tension, so do an adult's. Recent research indicates that emotional tears actually contain stress-related hormones, and crying is one way human beings can release pent-up frustration and feelings of helplessness. There's also scientific evidence supporting the age-old belief that people tend to feel better after a good cry. In a study of two hundred men and women who kept crying diaries for one month, 85 percent of the women and 73 percent of the men reported they felt better after crying. And the participants also noted a 40 percent reduction in stress after having a good cry.

19. Each parent should spend time alone, just to recoup, at least once a day (this is particularly important for Mom, who's likely to feel house- and baby-bound, since she's the one who spends her day caring for the colicky infant). Says Arlene, "It's absolutely essential to get out of the house for an hour every day. You can't physically and emotionally cope with a screaming baby without a break. You'll go crazy, and you won't be as effective in comforting your child as you would had you spent some time alone, regaining your perspective on things."

Arlene occasionally relied on her own mother to care for her colicky daughter, who cried most of the day—and night. "I believe a baby, especially one who's colicky and distraught, should be held a lot," she says, "and you need a second pair of 'loving arms' to do that carrying and comforting." Arlene, who's expecting her second child, maintains, "If *this* baby is colicky, I'll find the money somewhere to hire a baby nurse or part-time sitter to help get me through!"

Often, though, a parent will say, "If *I* can't stand the screaming, how can I expect someone else to, even a sitter who gets money for bearing up under it?" It's important to keep in mind that a grandparent, a sister, even a professional baby-sitter will often be able to tolerate a baby's constant screaming more easily than the baby's parents. A third party isn't as emotionally involved; she isn't questioning her parenting skills or constantly asking herself, "Am I doing something wrong?" or "Does the baby hate me?" Says Arlene, "My mother was very patient with the baby. When I couldn't cope, she'd take over and was able to get my daughter to fall asleep for *much longer* than my husband or I could."

Arrange for a relative or baby-sitter to take care of your infant for at least one hour a day (if finances permit, have someone sit for two or three hours; to manage this, breast-feeding mothers may need to introduce a "relief" bottle early on so the caretaker can feed the baby. You can either supplement with formula, or express your breast milk and store it in the refrigerator).

You may decide not to leave the house while someone else looks after your baby, opting to spend your time relaxing in your bathtub or, if the weather's nice, sitting in your backyard, enjoying a novel. It's best, though, to get away from the house so you can focus entirely on your own needs (that way, you won't be disturbed by your baby's cries). Take a long walk, go to an afternoon movie, visit a museum (truly a place of peace and quiet!), or arrange to meet a friend for lunch. You can even turn a trip to the grocery store (without baby, of course) into a pleasant outing. Says Maria, "Going grocery shopping while mom took care of my son was like a *vacation*. It was such a treat to be able to walk up and down the aisles and just look at the food, to do this simple thing and not hear my baby screaming."

20. Learn to accept help. No one expects you to be supermom or superdad, and you can't possibly do everything around the house and take care of baby at the same time. If a neighbor, relative, or friend offers to do your laundry, grocery shop, wash your car, mow your lawn—or take care of your baby—don't hesitate to say yes.

21. Eat well. You need to maintain your energy level, and a quick snack here and there won't carry you through the day—and nights, when you are up comforting baby. Eat three meals a day, with selections from the four basic food groups, and drink plenty of water (moms who are breast-feeding should ask their doctors for special dietary recommendations). Do snack on healthy foods like yogurt, cheese, whole-grain muffins, and fresh fruit, but forgo energy sappers such as coffee, tea (and other beverages containing caffeine), and sugar-laden foods.

If you find it's next to impossible to eat a full meal because of baby's wailing, keep a mechanical infant swing by your dinner table. Many parents report that swinging can mollify a baby for twenty minutes or longer.

22. Make "nighttime duty" interesting. If your baby routinely wakens during the night and requires an hour or more of comforting, buy or rent a videocassette player if you don't have one, and keep either rented or pretaped movies on hand for late-night viewing.

23. Streamline your life. Don't overburden yourself with nonessential tasks. No one expects a new parent —much less the parent of a colicky baby—to have a spic-and-span house. Learn to let some things go. If the kitchen isn't absolutely spotless, tell yourself that caring for your baby, or spending "alone time" or time with your partner, takes precedence over scrubbing the kitchen floor. You can also learn to ignore a few "dust bunnies" under the sofa, and the dinner dishes really don't need to be washed as soon as you get up from the table.

24. Organize your household for maximum efficiency. You may need to make changes in the two most important rooms, the kitchen and nursery. Everything in these two areas should be within easy reach to save you time and energy. For instance, if you routinely use a blender for meal preparation, but ordinarily keep it on an upper shelf, move it to a counter top. Rather

than storing pots and pans in hard-to-reach cupboards, hang them on wall racks so you don't waste time hunting for the right utensil. In the nursery, keep all the items you need for diapering and dressing near the changing table (some tables have underneath compartments or shelves for handy storage).

As you look around the rest of your house, you'll notice other areas that can be reorganized to save time and energy.

25. Although you'll probably welcome a weekly trip to the grocery store, don't try to do all the household errands yourself. Hire a high-school student or some other willing person to run errands for you on a regular basis.

26. Hire a junior-high or high-school student to take care of chores around the house. Says Arlene, "I had a high-school girl who did laundry for me twice a week, and it really helped."

A neighborhood teenager can also wash your car, mow the lawn, rake leaves and shovel snow, and help clean the house.

27. Divide "leftover" chores evenly. Once you've found a student to field chores and errands you and your partner aren't able to take care of, make an agreement to share the rest. Too often, it's the mother who's expected to cook dinner, clean the house, run errands, just because she's at home all day—while Dad's "out working." But no new mother should be

expected to manage everything—including a colicky baby—by herself.

The fairest way to divvy up chores is by assignment. Draw a chart, listing the chore or errand, the days it should be done, and agree between the two of you who does what. As you complete one task, check it off. If either of you falls behind, it's best not to criticize the forgetful partner. Both of you should merely make it a habit to check the chart every day. (Be sure to hang your work chart where you'll both see it, on a kitchen or bathroom wall, for instance.)

28. Take turns getting up during the night to feed or comfort baby. A nursing mom may wish to express and store breast milk, so Dad can give baby a bottle, or Dad can bring the baby to their bed, saving mom a trip to the nursery.

29. Relieve each other frequently. There's no need for both parents to try frantically to calm a screaming baby. You'll both feel better if Dad takes the baby for a half hour while Mom goes for a walk to reenergize herself, and vice versa.

30. Save time by cooking meals in bulk, then freezing them. On Sunday evening, prepare a big pot of chili or stew or soup, or several casserole dishes, divide into portions, and store in the freezer. Each evening simply heat the frozen entrée (a microwave oven can cut thawing/heating time). This way you won't spend hours in the kitchen each night as you try to comfort

your wailing baby at the same time. In addition, one-dish meals are both nutritious and timesaving.

31. Get an answering machine for your telephone. You can avoid calls at inconvenient times (when you're diapering baby or trying to catch up on your sleep), but still maintain contact with the outside world.

32. Nurture your relationship. All too often, the fatigue and stress parents of colicky babies experience fosters irritability and resentment that's aimed at each other. You may find yourselves quibbling about one another's parenting styles. Says one woman, "My husband and I bickered constantly about how the baby should be comforted, or how many times I should nurse her." Before a disagreement escalates into full-scale war, take a step back and agree not to criticize one another. Keep in mind that each partner will bring his own preconceived notions about parenting to the relationship, and one person's ideas are usually as valid as another's.

Rather than arguing when you're both tense and angry, agree to sit down and discuss whatever's bothering you when you're both calm. Often, by the time you do get around to talking about "the problem," you may not feel so strongly about it.

33. Admit your fears about your baby's health, as well as your own insecurities about your parenting abilities, to your partner and encourage one another to share concerns and doubts. Sometimes one partner sees the

other as "the strong one," and doesn't realize she or he has similar fears. By sharing your concerns, you keep the lines of communication open, you can comfort and empathize with one another, and avoid keeping painful feelings bottled up inside.

34. Arrange to spend time with your partner. As the baby becomes the focus of your attention, you and your spouse may find yourselves drifting apart, both physically and emotionally. It's likely, too, that you're both so tired, you stop listening to one another. One mother recalls her husband insisting he tell her all about his day at work; later she was surprised when he reacted angrily because she asked how his day had gone. She hadn't remembered a thing he'd said!

If possible, hire a baby-sitter one night a week and set that time aside for a "date" with your partner. Leave the house. Go to a movie or enjoy a leisurely dinner at a restaurant. Or indulge in a purely pleasurable—but frivolous—activity that takes your mind off baby. One dad tells of going miniature golfing with his wife. "We hadn't played miniature golf since we were in college together, but we needed some form of mindless recreation that would also help us connect again. We laughed so much during that hour, we forgot we'd practically been in tears forty-five minutes earlier because our daughter wouldn't stop squalling!"

It's also helpful to set aside time each day—twenty or thirty minutes—to be with your partner. When your baby finally falls asleep, sit on the sofa or bed together and snuggle. This sounds old-fashioned, but by touching each other, by being physically close, you give each other emotional support. Many parents note, too, the importance of sharing humor, of laughing together, in order to keep their spirits up during baby's colicky phase. (Recent research indicates that hearty laughter promotes good mental and physical health—and relieves stress and tension.) If you have a VCR, rent funny movies or tape reruns of "I Love Lucy" and watch these shows together when you're feeling down. Or read humorous passages from books to each other. One mom remembers reading chapters from James Herriot's book *All Creatures Great and Small* to her husband. "Herriot is a hilarious writer," she says, "and we looked forward to our 'nightly' chapter. His books could crack us up, even when we'd had a particularly rough day and were convinced we might never laugh again!"

8. Does Colic Harm Your Baby?

One of the major concerns of parents of colicky babies is that the condition will, somehow, affect their child adversely years later. After all, they ask, how can a tiny baby endure so much misery and distress during a crucial developmental state and not show any serious, long-term effects?

Although few studies have been done to ascertain whether colic has any aftereffects (partly because it's extremely difficult to follow formerly colicky babies for the next seventy or so years!), the general assumption—based on testimony from thousands of doctors and parents—is that once the colic has passed, colicky babies grow up to be just as happy, healthy, and "normal" as children who didn't have the condition during infancy. There is also a growing body of evidence that colicky, or "difficult," babies may, possibly, be superior in cognitive and social skills, thanks to the constant stimulation and attention they receive from their parents!

As mentioned earlier, your colicky baby is probably experiencing some pain, most likely in the gastrointestinal tract, as a result of abdominal contractions and "gulped air" that triggers gassiness. And, too, she's definitely in "psychological" or emotional distress, but her unhappiness may be due to a number of factors, including pain, loss of equilibrium or a feeling of being "out of control," and a general sense of being overwhelmed because she can't cope with the external and internal stimuli she's constantly bombarded with. As the parent of a colicky baby, it is natural for you to feel upset when your infant seems to be going through a "living hell" during these early, critical months. But remember that even the infant with the severest case of colic, the one who cries for most of the day, does have her "good times." Says Laura, "Although my daughter was miserable the majority of the time, when she slept she had the most beautiful smiles. I think she was having good dreams—and that reassured me that something was right, that she had an hour of happiness here and there."

A father who claims to remember being "less than a year old and standing up in my crib," wonders if his colicky daughter might have flashbacks, or memories later on about her terrible bout with colic. Psychologists do theorize that we human beings harbor even our earliest memories in the deep recesses of our brains, and if that's true, we can hypothesize that for-

merly colicky children have, tucked away in their
memory bank, snippets of their excruciating colicky
months. But it's unlikely that those memories ever surface. Ask a child or adult who was severely colicky if
he remembers how traumatic his first three months of
life were, and he's likely to shrug his shoulders and
reply, "Well, Mom and Dad say I screamed bloody
murder and was doubled up in pain, but you'll have to
take their word for it. I can't remember a thing!" In
fact, older children and adults are surprised to hear
they gave their parents such a rough time. Says Leah,
"I think I was basically an easygoing kid, but my
mother insists there were times when she was at the
end of her rope because I *supposedly* had colic. I just
can't imagine myself as a screamer, though. I never
even had temper tantrums when I was a toddler and
preschooler!"

Some researchers have attempted to link infant
colic to future gastrointestinal problems, while others
hypothesize that colicky babies grow up to beget colicky babies. A handful of experts also feel that parents
of colicky babies are themselves prone to gastrointestinal problems, but the evidence is sparse.

Although the theory that formerly colicky babies
are more likely to produce colicky babies is intriguing,
no one has proven it. Most of the parents we talked to
reported that they were not colicky as infants (two
mothers were, and wondered if their children had "in-
herited" the tendency). Essentially, researchers have
found that a parent who was colicky is no more likely
to have a colicky infant than a parent who didn't have

colic. It is possible, however, for a parent who is lactose intolerant (unable to digest the sugars in cow's milk) to pass the tendency—and related colicky symptoms—on to his or her child.

There's limited evidence that parents of colicky babies have a history of gastrointestinal problems themselves. Most of the parents interviewed for this book felt their digestive systems functioned "normally," though two mothers noted they had gastrointestinal difficulties. Says Carol, who was recently diagnosed as having an ulcer, "I don't know if my stomach problem has anything to do with my son's colic, especially since the ulcer didn't develop until I was in my twenties." Another mother adds, "I was a colicky baby myself, and even now when I'm under a lot of stress, I have bouts of diarrhea and cramping."

Are colicky babies more likely than other babies to develop gastrointestinal problems during their childhood? The evidence is spotty and conflicting, and some parents will tell you their child has no problem with cramping, gassiness, diarrhea, or constipation, while others maintain their child definitely has stomach problems. Carol reports that her son, now five, "gets diarrhea attacks whenever he plays a lot and is overly excited. He's not in any pain, though, and the gastroenterologist I took him to diagnosed Michael as having irritable bowel syndrome. The doctor thinks it's a passing phase and didn't link it to the colic."

Leah, who's in her forties—and had severe colic for five months—feels her babyhood condition "has continued right into adulthood. My mother says I was 'born constipated' and apparently I was always very gassy. A few years ago when I was having heartburn and stomach cramps a doctor diagnosed my condition as an 'extended case of colic'! He laughed when he said it, but he added that I had all the symptoms, just like a baby."

At least one prominent colic researcher feels that colicky babies have an increased susceptibility to "sleep disorders" in later infancy and childhood. However, most experts agree that those babies who have trouble sleeping through the night once their colic has passed are "conditioned" to avoid falling asleep—or to awaken several times during the night—because they're so used to a parent's constant attempts to get them to doze off or to being comforted when they suddenly wake up. (We'll talk about getting your postcolicky baby to sleep through the night in chapter 11.)

Over the years, researchers have tried to prove that colicky babies grow into hyperactive children, but there seems to be no link between the two conditions. Although one parent we talked with described her son as "more nervous than other kids," other moms and dads said their children were generally easygoing and adaptable. Says Alice, "Nancy is intelligent and high-spirited, but she's not the least bit hyperactive."

Some childhood researchers feel that colicky babies are more likely to become "difficult" as they grow older. This notion persists and is based primarily on one landmark study in which colic researcher W. B. Carey tracked a small group of colicky infants. When the children were old enough to be given the Carey

Treatment Profile (after their colic had subsided), they were rated as following: four were deemed "difficult," four as "almost difficult," four as "almost easy," and one as "easy." Carey felt that the significant concentration in the first two groups suggested the strong possibility of a link between colic and difficult temperament. However, the Carey sample is too small to draw any definite conclusions from, and it's also possible that some of the infants Carey tested were not only colicky—but happened to be born with difficult temperaments as well. Common sense—and firsthand testimony from parents—tells us that colicky babies don't necessarily turn into "difficult" toddlers and pre-schoolers. Too many parents say that once colic has subsided, the infant metamorphoses into a happy, easygoing baby. "A totally different personality emerged once my son's colic ended," says Tess. "Overnight he became a wonderful, beaming baby, and at age five he's still got that delightful personality."

The good—and surprising—news is that colicky babies may actually benefit from their turbulent first few months. Numerous studies show that because these babies are carried and "stimulated" more by their parents, they may develop superior cognitive and social skills or mature faster intellectually. In fact, one researcher has found that children who were held a great deal during infancy showed superior cognitive development when tested eight years later.

In a recent Canadian study, researchers found that difficult babies, the ones who cried persistently in early infancy, grew up to be smarter than their more placid counterparts. The research team divided seventy-five babies into groups according to temperament: difficult, easy, and average. The difficult babies were those with coliclike symptoms, including irritability, intense emotional reactions, an inability to handle new stimuli, and a tendency to be unsoothable. When the children reached four-and-a-half years of age, the researchers administered intelligence tests, and the "difficults" scored significantly higher than the easy and average kids. The researchers theorized that parents tend to give more time and attention to difficult, demanding babies than to easygoing infants who are able to soothe themselves. This constant interaction between parent and baby, the parent's singing and talking or trying to distract the infant with rattles and other toys as well as sights and sounds, seems to speed up the child's intellectual development. All the parents we talked to noted that their formerly colicky children seemed especially bright. Says Carol, "My son's teacher thinks he's smarter than the other kids in his class." Alice says her daughter is "a class leader." And another mother notes that her two-year-old daughter has "an amazingly large vocabulary and has already learned to dress herself!"

9. Can Colic Affect Your Future Relationship with Your Child?

Most experts agree that colic is a condition that affects the parents just as much as the baby—and how parents weather their child's colicky phase, how they react to or perceive the irritable, inconsolable infant, can set the foundation for the future parent/child relationship.

In chapter 1 we talked about the profoundly disturbing effect a crying infant has on her parents. A baby's wail can make our heart rate skyrocket, our muscles tense up, our palms sweat. A screaming, unsoothable infant can shake our confidence in ourselves as parents. Although most moms and dads realize deep down that they'll "grow out" of their own period of "colicky parenthood" when their baby outgrows *her* colicky phase, they have to admit that parenting the colicky baby is full of emotional pitfalls: it can be frustrating because they often feel as though their child is manipulating them or turning her back on them when they try to help her, or condemning them for not being "perfect parents."

Feelings of anger and hurt are both common and quite natural, but when parents find themselves experiencing these same feelings months or years after the colic crisis is over, they're surprised. Many parents of formerly colicky children experience "colic flash-backs" as feelings of anger, resentment, and hurt crop up again when their baby is well past her colicky stage. If they felt that baby was trying to manipulate them with her cries during the colicky period, they may tend to perceive her cries negatively during her toddler-hood. If they're trying to teach her how to eat solid foods—and she consistently spits her strained carrots at them—they may get mad, thinking baby is once again rebelling against their parental authority. And when she's two and becoming fiercely independent, trying to separate from them and define herself as a unique human being, they may feel as though she's rejecting them (much like she "rejected" them during her more unresponsive colicky months).

To avoid parent/child conflicts where parents and toddler (or preschooler) pit themselves against one an-other in a battle of wills or the parents feel like "fail-ures" or as though they're being rejected whenever a colicky flashback occurs, they need to step back and get in touch with what they're feeling and why (most likely, negative emotions can be linked to feelings ex-perienced during the child's colicky phase). Once par-ents accept that they're frustrated or hurt or angry, they can then try to view the child's behavior in the context of what's happening *now*, in relation to the child's developmental stage. (For instance, the baby who spits her food at you may not yet have learned how to swallow properly. She's not angry at you or rejecting you or your authority; she's just trying to deal with learning a new skill.)

While carrying a few negative emotions over into the postcolicky months is almost inevitable, a serious parent/child problem can develop when parents view their colicky babies so negatively that they "turn off" to them. There is evidence that some mothers of difficult, persistently crying babies attempt to desensitize themselves to the sound of the baby's cries, that they react nonemotionally to the baby's demands and, over a period of weeks or months, become less responsive than mothers of more placid babies. Unless the parent receives help, such as family counseling or private therapy, it's possible that she may inadvertently desensitize herself in other areas of social interaction with her child as well. For example, when the baby smiles at his mother, she may not react positively; instead of smiling back at him, she might turn away, or ignore, or not even notice his grin. The mother has begun to perceive her baby so negatively she may be unable to establish a close, positive relationship with him, and as a result, both mother and child will fail to benefit from the mutual exchange of positive, loving behaviors. If this type of relationship continues after the colicky stage has passed, both parent and child are in for a rocky time. They may never connect in a natural, responsive way.

Of course, the worst-case scenario of a parent/child

relationship gone wrong is one where the child is physically abused. There's increasing evidence that difficult babies may be at greater risk of child abuse than more easygoing infants, and several studies indicate that babies who have a high-pitched, screeching cry can trigger batterings by parents. Research also shows that abusive parents—rather than reacting *non*emotionally to their child—tend to be more intense in their reactions and, instead of ignoring a crying infant, may lash out at him. What's more, they tend to perceive both a baby's negative—and positive—behaviors as demanding. For instance, an abusive father may see his child's cry *and* smile as asking him for some sort of attention he's not prepared, or willing, to give. And rather than feeling sympathy for a crying infant, or a combination of empathy and annoyance, the abusive parent is more likely to feel only anger. (Of course, many factors besides a child's cries play into child abuse. Financial and marital difficulties, addiction to drugs or alcohol, very low self-esteem on the part of one or both parents, depression, a mother's extreme sense of isolation, a history of being abused as a child, and ambivalence about becoming parents—any of these situations, or a combination of several, may lay the groundwork for batterings. Parents who are facing problems such as these, and feel they might harm their children, should seek professional help immediately.)

The "densensitized parent" and the abusive mother or father are, of course, the extremes, but all parents of colicky babies will—at one time or another—find themselves reverting to "colicky parenthood" attitudes. It's important to keep in mind, though, that like any other parent, you shouldn't feel guilty because you heartily dislike certain things about your child's behavior. It's perfectly normal to dislike the fact that a baby cries from 8:00 P.M. until 2:00 A.M. (or that he obstinately shouts *"No!"* at us during the terrible twos)—and yet still love him. Often, our great expectations about how we and our children *should* be get in the way of parenting. Once we accept the reality that both we and our children are perfectly imperfect and will be that way for the rest of the parent/child relationship, we can begin to relax and balance both the frustrations and joys of parenthood.

10. Looking Ahead

"Colic is like labor. You go through the most excruciating pain, but when it's over you tend to forget what it was like." So says Alice, whose formerly colicky daughter is now a precocious, outgoing preschooler.

While parents of postcolicky children are quick to tell you their experience was "horrible, unimaginably brutal," they also often have trouble remembering the minute details of their child's colicky phase. The endless nights spent comforting baby blur together, and once parents and child are past the colicky period, parents begin to focus on the here and now, they react to their child "in the present." For example, if you're sick at heart because your three-week-old son cries incessantly (and you're secretly worried he may have something more serious than colic), you can reassure yourself that within the next few months, when your baby's colic subsides, your focus will be on something entirely new and unrelated to his upsetting condition. When you first introduce your baby to solid foods, for instance, and he's smiling at you, "asking" for another spoonful of rice cereal, you may have difficulty believing this is the same baby who pushed away your breast so vehemently just a few months earlier because he was too agitated to nurse!

"Essentially," says Bob, "you gain a lot of perspective *after* your child's colic has passed. The trick is to try to keep perspective on things *during* the colicky phase." Bob is the father of two colicky babies, and the second time around he had "a much easier time coping with the baby's condition. My wife and I had lived through the trauma of our daughter, Nancy's, colic, and during that time we often felt it would never end. But it did, and I think that's what helped us achieve real perspective during our second daughter's colicky period. We knew from our firsthand experience with Nancy that Marissa would emerge from the colic within about three months, that it *would end*. We also knew that kids didn't die from colic and that the condition doesn't seem to affect their emotional or mental health. Nancy turned out just fine. She's a bright, happy child, and based on that knowledge, we realized Marissa would be fine, too."

Several parents we talked to admitted they harbored some reservations about having a second child after caring for a colicky one. But they gave themselves a few years to "forget the painful, colicky months," then decided to add to their families. Still, once you've weathered the stormy colicky period, it's only natural to feel some hesitation about having another child, lest that one turn out to be colicky, too. Says Matt, "Tess and I had one noncolicky child, and she was really content with being the mother of an 'only.' But I definitely wanted a brother or sister for my son, and I convinced Tess that we should have another baby.

"Of course, Thomas turned out to be colicky! It was a nightmare. If Thomas had been our firstborn, I might have acquiesced to my wife's ambivalence about having more than one child, and we'd have had just the one."

Some parents voice the fear that their "bond" with their colicky baby may not be strong enough because the child seems to relate so little to them during those early months. "My son and I didn't bond until his colic was over," says Maria. "It was impossible to cuddle him, to connect with him. He was so miserable he didn't want to be held, didn't smile. He just screamed." Another mother adds, "Whenever I read magazine articles saying how important early bonding is—from the very moment of birth, it seems!—I feel a little sad. It's very hard to bond in the usual way with a colicky baby, one who's so easily startled and spends most of her day crying. But my daughter and I did have our times of closeness, especially when she nursed or when she calmed down long enough for me to cuddle her. She often slept between my husband and me in our bed, too. We all felt very close during those times."

Matt feels he and his son are especially close today because of "the many hours we spent together when he was colicky. I think we bonded during those early months; we were together so much of the time when he was in distress, and I feel that when you comfort a baby to that degree you're truly bonding with him.

"I'd give Thomas a bottle at night, then lie on my back and hold him against my chest, rubbing his back for hours," adds Matt. "Even today, he likes to be physically close to me, wrestling on the floor, for instance. The kid is all over me!"

Maria's mother spent many days and weeks comforting her grandson, and Maria feels that as a result the two are "incredibly close. It's as though my son senses that he spent much of his time in this woman's loving arms. Whenever she visits, he's the first one out of the door, shouting, 'Grandma's here!' He spends most of his time with her when she comes."

Tess echoes Maria's sentiment that a colicky baby will develop a special bond with the person—or people—who comforted her. "I was colicky myself," she remembers, "and apparently I cried nonstop. My father was very attentive. He held me, rocked me, carried me, danced with me. I've always had an especially close relationship with him. And perhaps that's because—despite what I put him through with my screaming—he tells me to this day, 'I fell in love with you!'"

11. Helping Your Postcolic Baby Sleep Through the Night

Though some formerly colicky babies fall miraculously into a peaceful nighttime sleep pattern once their condition subsides, many postcolic infants resist going to sleep at bedtime and waken numerous times during the wee hours, just as they did during their colicky months. Experts feel these babies are "conditioned" to avoid falling asleep as well as to waking up frequently during the night. After all, they've become accustomed to having Mom or Dad carry or rock or sing to them—and in extreme cases, bundle them up and take them for a midnight car ride! They're also used to being comforted several times during the night, and they now wake up as if on cue, expecting Mom or Dad to keep them company.

Between the ages of three and five months, it's wise

to help your baby learn how to fall asleep at a pre-scribed hour and to sleep through the night. This means giving up the familiar colic comforters you and baby have relied on: endless hours of walking and rocking baby, as well as frequent nighttime feedings. Although we don't advocate a "cold turkey" approach to helping your baby master nighttime sleeping (few parents can—or should—harden their hearts, shut the nursery door, and let baby cry her lungs out), we do feel that the baby who's comforted every time she whimpers during the night may need that type of at-tention for months—or years—to come. Mary, two and a half, regularly wakens several times during the night, crying for her mother's comforting arms. Her frustrated mom admits she never helped Mary learn how to fall asleep unassisted, but immediately went to her crib, picked her up, and cuddled her whenever she began to cry or call out. This mother now has a four-month-old son who's already learned how to sleep through the night. "It took only a couple of weeks," she says, "and I can't believe how simple it was. If only I'd helped Mary in the same way!"

Once your baby's colicky stage passes, you're still bound to waken when you hear the whimper or cry, fearful that she's about to launch into a tirade. Re-member, though, that babies tend to make "sleep sounds" during the night. They whimper and cry a lit-tle, then become quiet again. Although it's fine to check on your little sleep-talker, just to make sure she's okay, don't pick her up. That's her cue to come awake.

By the age of three months, a few babies will sleep a full eight to ten hours, though most will waken after about four hours of sleep, fuss for a while, then go back to sleep for another four hours. But if your postcolic baby is a conditioned nighttime crier, you'll need to help her learn how to fall—and stay—asleep.

1. Start by reducing the number of hours baby sleeps during the day. A baby who's had two long naps and a few short ones is more likely to be ready to play come bedtime! Also, make sure she's properly stimulated during the day. A trip to the park, a few minutes in her mechanical infant swing, frequent attention from you (talking, singing, introducing her to new, interesting toys) will help her work off energy. A bored, inactive baby can store up energy, tension, and resist falling asleep or waken frequently during the night.

2. Make sure baby is well fed before bedtime. Feed her at 10:00 or 11:00 P.M., even if you must waken her to do so. If she misses this nighttime feeding, you can bet she'll wake up at 2:00 A.M., ravenous and crying.

3. Give your baby a "security toy," a soft, plush animal, for instance. This cuddly pal should be left in baby's crib so she begins to associate it with bedtime and sleeptime. She'll find comfort in her crib pal when Mom or Dad isn't in the room.

4. Establish a regular bedtime routine that lasts from ten to twenty minutes. You may want to bathe baby to

warm and soothe her, then hold her on your lap while you sing to her.

5. When baby begins to show signs of tiredness (yawning, squirming), put her in her crib and let her fall asleep there, not in your arms. This way she'll learn to doze off in her bed; otherwise she may continue to rely on you to hold her for an hour or more until she dozes off.

6. Between the ages of two and three months, many babies become wary of darkness. If your baby seems alarmed when you turn out the lights in her room, keep a soft night light on.

7. Once your baby is in her crib, rub her back gently, give her a goodnight kiss or say "good night" softly, then leave the room. If she cries, return to the room, stroke her gently for a few minutes, then repeat your "good night," and leave. (You may need to do this several times.)

8. You can expect your baby to wail in protest for the first few nights. But remember, too, that many babies need a little cry time (five or ten minutes) to unwind before they go to sleep.

9. Your baby will most likely waken several times during the night for the first week or so until she becomes accustomed to her new sleep schedule. When she wakens, go to her crib but don't pick her up. Instead,

talk softly and reassuringly to her, gently stroking her back. Then leave the room.

10. During subsequent nights, each time baby wakens, lengthen your response time. Wait three minutes before going to her on the second night, five minutes on the third, eight minutes on the fourth, and so on. This will give her a chance to use her own self-soothing techniques such as thumb or finger sucking.

11. By this time, you're well acquainted with your baby's cries. If she suddenly emits a sharp, piercing "pain" cry during the night, obviously you should go to her immediately, pick her up, and check for fever or other symptoms of illness. If her cry is a persistent distress signal, telling you she's in discomfort, check for wetness. You can change a semi-awake, fussing baby in her crib rather than carrying her to the changing table (and fully waking her!); then stroke her and talk reassuringly to her.

Helping your postcolic baby learn how to sleep through the night can take anywhere from a few days to a few weeks. But by being consistent and patient, by sticking to the routine you've set, you and your child will eventually sleep through the night "like a baby."

12. Questions Parents Ask: A Review

Is colic a disease?

Colic is not a disease or illness, that is, it's not caused by germs or bacteria—and the colicky baby isn't "sick." Rather, colic is a short-lived condition affecting between 20 and 30 percent of all infants.

What causes colic?

No one knows for certain, but we do have a pretty good idea. Experts feel that a subgroup of colicky babies (possibly 30 to 35 percent) are unable to digest the sugars or proteins in cow's-milk formula (in breast-fed babies, the infants may be sensitive to dairy products the mother ingests and passes through her milk). But symptoms in the majority of colicky babies are believed to be caused by an immaturity of the central nervous system (CNS). (Actually all babies are born with "immature" nervous systems, but the colicky baby's CNS is less well developed than that of the non-colicky infant.) It takes time for a colicky baby's nervous system to "settle into place," and while the CNS regulates itself, the baby's brain may send inappropriate messages to the various parts of the body. An immature CNS can trigger spasms or reactions in any of the baby's nerves or muscles: the abdominal muscles may contract violently, causing cramping, or the baby's arms and legs might suddenly go rigid or begin to flail around wildly, while the helpless infant is unable to regain control. And because the baby's CNS isn't functioning smoothly yet, he can become overwhelmed by both external and internal stimuli, going crazy at the slightest sight or sound, such as a flashing light or the growling of his own stomach.

Parents should be reassured that in time, their infants' CNS will develop and mature, and within a few months the baby will begin to have more control over his body and be able to process stimuli more effectively.

How long does colic usually last?

Generally, colic begins within five to ten days after a baby's birth and persists for approximately three months (hence, the Chinese term for colic, "hundred-days crying," or the Western version, "three-month colic"). Some babies show symptoms of colic as early as the first or second day, however, and many colic cases last as long as four to six months. Colic symptoms that persist past the sixth month may be due to an undetected food allergy.

Is there a cure for colic?

At present, there's no "cure" for colic. In the severest cases of the condition, doctors have prescribed various medications (usually sedatives or muscle relaxants) to ease the symptoms, but the drugs do have side effects and are not the preferred method of treatment. Rather, most parents and pediatricians choose the many noninvasive remedies that help calm the agitated infant, such as taking the baby for car rides, massaging her tummy, or distracting her with singing, dancing, rocking, and swinging.

How can I tell for certain if my baby has colic—or if he's just "fussy"?

There's no medical "test" for colic. That is, evidence of the condition won't show up on an X ray or in a blood test. Frequently, pediatricians misdiagnose colicky babies as "fussy" or overly irritable, while fussy babies are sometimes diagnosed as colicky.

Once your doctor has examined your baby to rule out any underlying medical conditions that could account for the child's crying (an ear or urinary-tract infection, for example), she will need a detailed description of your baby's symptoms and behavior in order to make a definite diagnosis. In general, colicky babies cry excessively (more than three hours a day) and are inconsolable; that is, once they're picked up or diapered or fed, they fail to quiet down for more than a few minutes.

They are extremely sensitive to the slightest touch, sight, or sound and may start to cry uncontrollably if someone brushes up against them or they hear the faint clatter of a cup being dropped two rooms away! Because they're so sensitive to stimuli, colicky babies startle more often than other babies; a sudden noise may cause them to stiffen and arch their backs, thrusting their arms and legs outward as if to grab on to something. This is a part of their "colicky body language," which often includes wild thrashing of their tiny arms and legs. Colicky babies also appear to suffer from abdominal pain, pulling their legs tightly up to their distended bellies, often after they've eaten.

Does my baby feel pain during a colic attack?

We don't know for certain what sensations a colicky baby experiences during the throes of a colic attack, but it's likely that she feels both physical pain as well as emotional distress. Infants with colic are believed to have extremely low sensory thresholds, and the colicky baby may perceive a gas bubble as excruciating while his placid counterpart won't be fazed at all by a gassy tummy. The colicky baby seems to experience every sensation more acutely than other babies do; so, even though the discomfort he feels might not be severe, to him it's unbearable.

This doesn't mean that a colicky baby is in pain at

all times during a colic attack. He may be in *emotional* distress instead, because he's overly stimulated or "strung out."

What types of remedies work best to soothe a colicky child?

Parents report that two types of colic management techniques are particularly effective: those that soothe a baby's gassy or crampy tummy, and those that are rhythmic, helping to distract the infant from his woes. The first type includes everything from tummy massages to exerting gentle pressure on the abdomen to warming the baby's belly with a warm hot-water bottle wrapped in a towel. The second type includes car rides, dancing with, rocking, or swinging baby, or providing him with certain types of soothing music or "white noise," such as the sound of a vacuum cleaner or whirring fan. For a complete discussion of colic remedies, see chapter 6.

Can colic harm my baby?

Experts feel that colic has no adverse, long-term physical, mental, or emotional side effects. Some research indicates that colicky babies may be more prone to gastrointestinal problems as they grow older (possibly into adulthood), but there's no definite proof. A colicky infant is normal and healthy in every way according to the most recent research. She will develop physically and socially at the same rate as other babies, and recent studies suggest that formerly colicky children may actually be smarter than their noncolicky counterparts. Because of all the stimulation they receive from their parents during their early months, these babies may develop superior cognitive and motor skills.

Studies also show that colicky infants are no more likely than noncolicky babies to be "difficult" or hyperactive as they grow older.

Index

About the Author

Phyllis Schneider is a freelance writer/editor and former editor-in-chief of *YM* magazine. She writes frequently about parenting and health issues, and her articles have appeared in many national publications, including *Parents*, *Working Woman*, *Woman's Day*, *Expecting*, and *Redbook*. She lives in Crestwood, New York, with her husband Ted and daughter Brooke, and dogs Duffy and Toby.

Parents® MAGAZINE
READ ALOUD
BOOK CLUB

READING ALOUD—the loving, personal gift for you and your child to share.

Children's reading experts agree . . . reading aloud offers the easiest, most effective way to turn your child into a lifelong reader. And, it's as much fun for you as it is for your child.

Easy access to a variety of such important "first" books (read-aloud books) has presented a major problem for busy parents. And a challenge that *Parents* Magazine was well suited to undertake.

The result—a book club that can be your child's *first club*. A club for sharing and reading aloud. An early reading habit to last a lifetime, with books designed, created and published solely for this purpose. *Parents* Magazine Read Aloud Book Club.

If you're a concerned parent, and would like more information about our club and your free gift, just fill in the coupon below, and mail it in.